SWITHEART

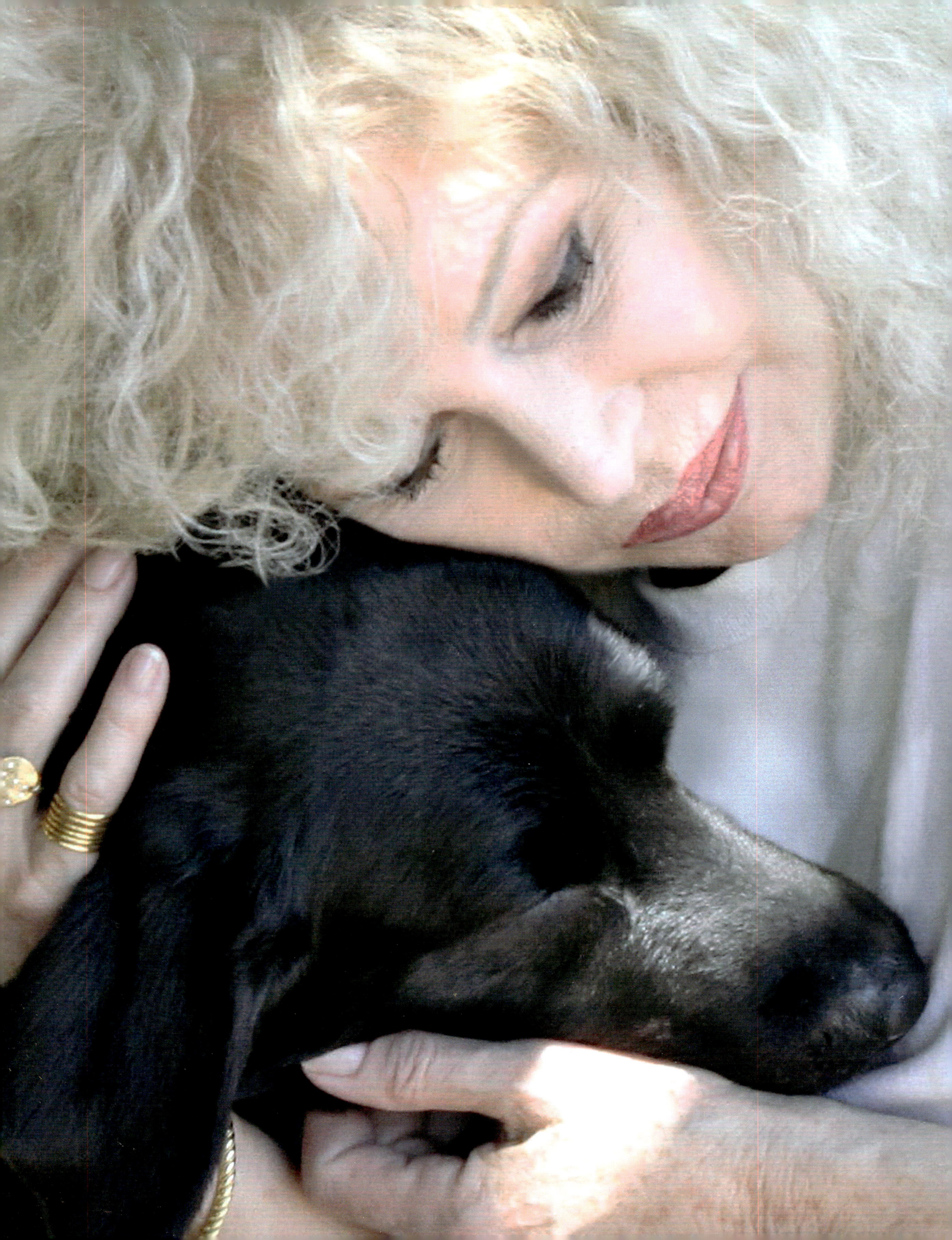

CONTENTS

ACKNOWLEDGEMENTS

First and foremost I must give special thanks to my friend John Yurtchuk, without whom my books would not become reality.

Concept, Design, Artwork, and Writing, by Loretta Swit

Artwork Scans by Duggal, New York

This book is dedicated to the safety, protection and care of all animals, as well as the preservation of their natural habitats.

Gandhi said that you can judge nations by the way their animals are treated. Herein lies the artwork of relentless animal rescue and protection.

Website: www.switheart.org

Instagram: @lorettaswit

Facebook: RealLorettaSwit

Twitter: @Loretta_Swit

Cameo.com/lorettaswit

INTRODUCTION FROM MIKE FARELL

I want to welcome you to the experience of Loretta Swit's embrace.

Lorette describes herself in these pages as having had a life-long "need for self-expression." She's correct, of course, but the term is open to misinterpretation. The idea of 'self' expression can suggest someone who feels unheard and wants and needs your attention. Those of us lucky enough to know this woman and to bask in the glow of her affection see all too clearly that what she possesses and feels the need to express is an almost overwhelming love of life and all living things.

Those who benefit from the proceeds of this book speak a language few besides Lorette can understand, so while they're unlikely to read the book they can certainly sense that her love for them expresses itself in generosity, both personal generosity and a generosity of spirit. For the rest of us this generosity is known to produce wonderful entertainments, whether in the form of beautiful personal moments of warmth, deeply moving dramatic portrayals, riotously funny comedy scenes, songs, dances or simply a sparkling smile, as a result of which we, her friends and her fans — all of whom are thought of as friends — are enriched, lifted up, better for the experience.

Lorette's art, warm, personal, and imbued with the loving energy that characterizes her every act, takes many forms. I've watched, dazzled, as she carefully needle pointed something wonderful for a friend in the spare moments available between the scenes of a television show, and I've sat in the audience, enthralled, as she magically brought characters to life on stage, educating and exhilarating us in the process.

One is made to wonder if there's a limit to the forms in which this 'need' of hers can express itself. The answer is certainly that we don't yet know.

Today the works you'll enjoy in these pages are simply yet another dimension of Loretta's loving embrace, this one specifically intended to share her wonder at the beauty and glory of — and affinity with — the animal kingdom, while at the same time enabling a better, safer, more appreciated life for so many of her treasured friends who are too often overlooked or forgotten.

Enjoy.

Mike Farrell

TO MY READERS

This book is a full-circle journey of self-expression. As early as six years old, I loved to draw and just plain doodle. When I saw an ad for an art contest in a magazine, I begged my mother to enter my drawing. Relenting, she submitted my sketch, and I won the contest! I must have been driven by a need for self-expression, which ultimately, has defined my life.

A voracious reader, I sometimes went through a book a day, while 'acting out' all the characters in the books. I'd learn later in drama class that I had actually been 'in rehearsal' since childhood. We lived in a neighborhood where singing was believed to be praying twice. Naturally, I sang in the choir. I studied tap and ballet dancing. I became a majorette. I was a cheerleader. I was 'out there' being me, or rather, expressing the me I wanted to become – painting posters for school, drawing my own greeting cards. Performing in and directing school plays. My serious study of theatre was a natural segue, but my artwork continued unabated.

Painting was an immense joy, but I didn't regard it as something anyone would consider important, until a very dear friend, the wonderful actress Madlyn Rhue, changed all that. One evening, we were to have dinner, and she was running late.
With humor, she thrust a large drawing pad at me with the suggestion that I amuse myself while she hurried to get ready. When she reappeared, ready to go, I handed her the drawing pad with my sketch. She was dumbfounded... having had no idea I'd been doodling and sketching all my life. She framed and kept the sketch, and was so impressed that she gifted me with an artist's easel at Christmas.

Inevitably, my passion for animals and my work in the humane environment merged with my watercolors. I owe so much to my friends for their support, for seeing the value of my efforts in ways I did not.
John Yurtchuk, friend extraordinaire, so generous and loving. Not only do I get his friendship, but I also benefit from his expertise. I have learned much from him — his nurturing has brought out the best in me.

Loretta Swit, September 2016

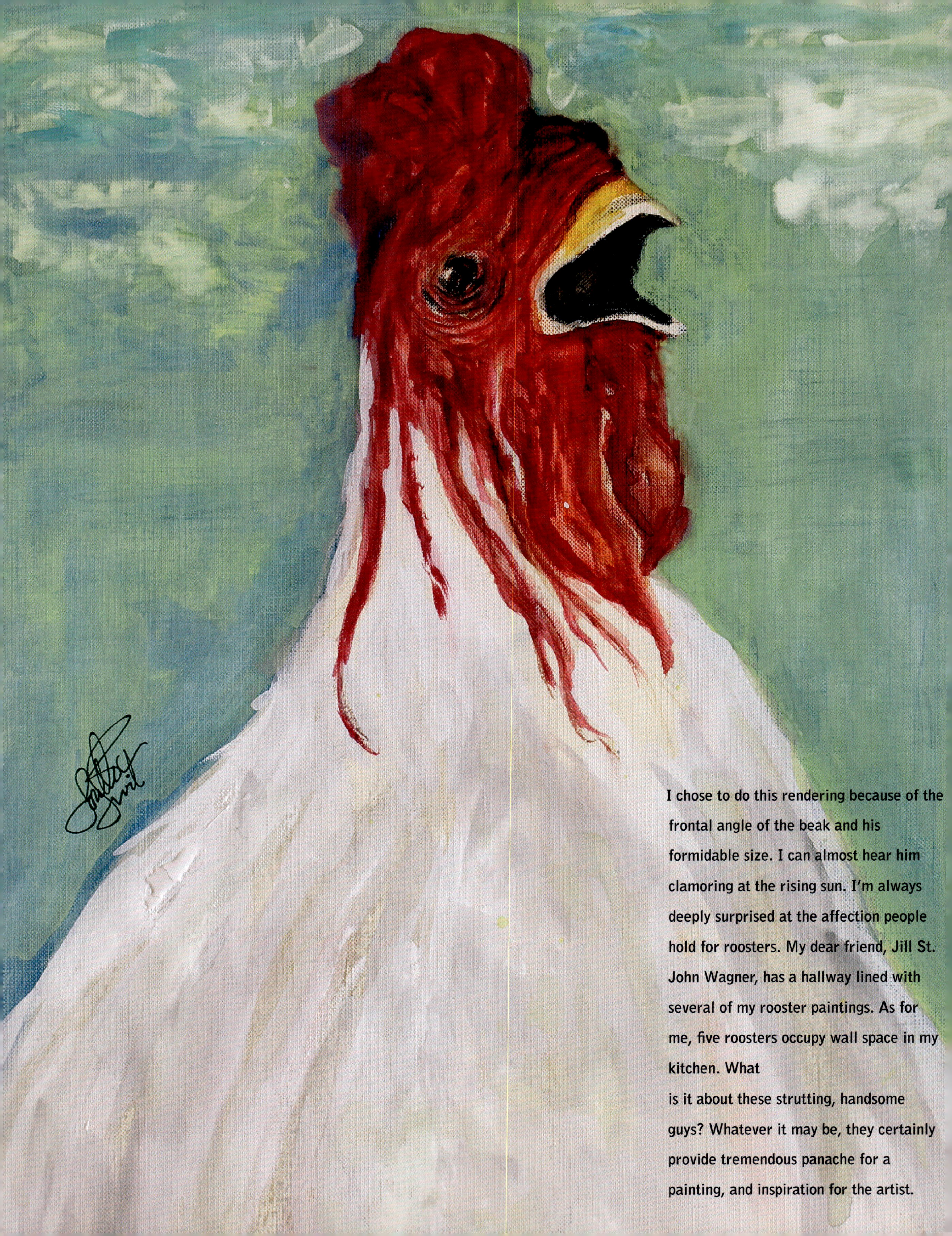

I chose to do this rendering because of the frontal angle of the beak and his formidable size. I can almost hear him clamoring at the rising sun. I'm always deeply surprised at the affection people hold for roosters. My dear friend, Jill St. John Wagner, has a hallway lined with several of my rooster paintings. As for me, five roosters occupy wall space in my kitchen. What is it about these strutting, handsome guys? Whatever it may be, they certainly provide tremendous panache for a painting, and inspiration for the artist.

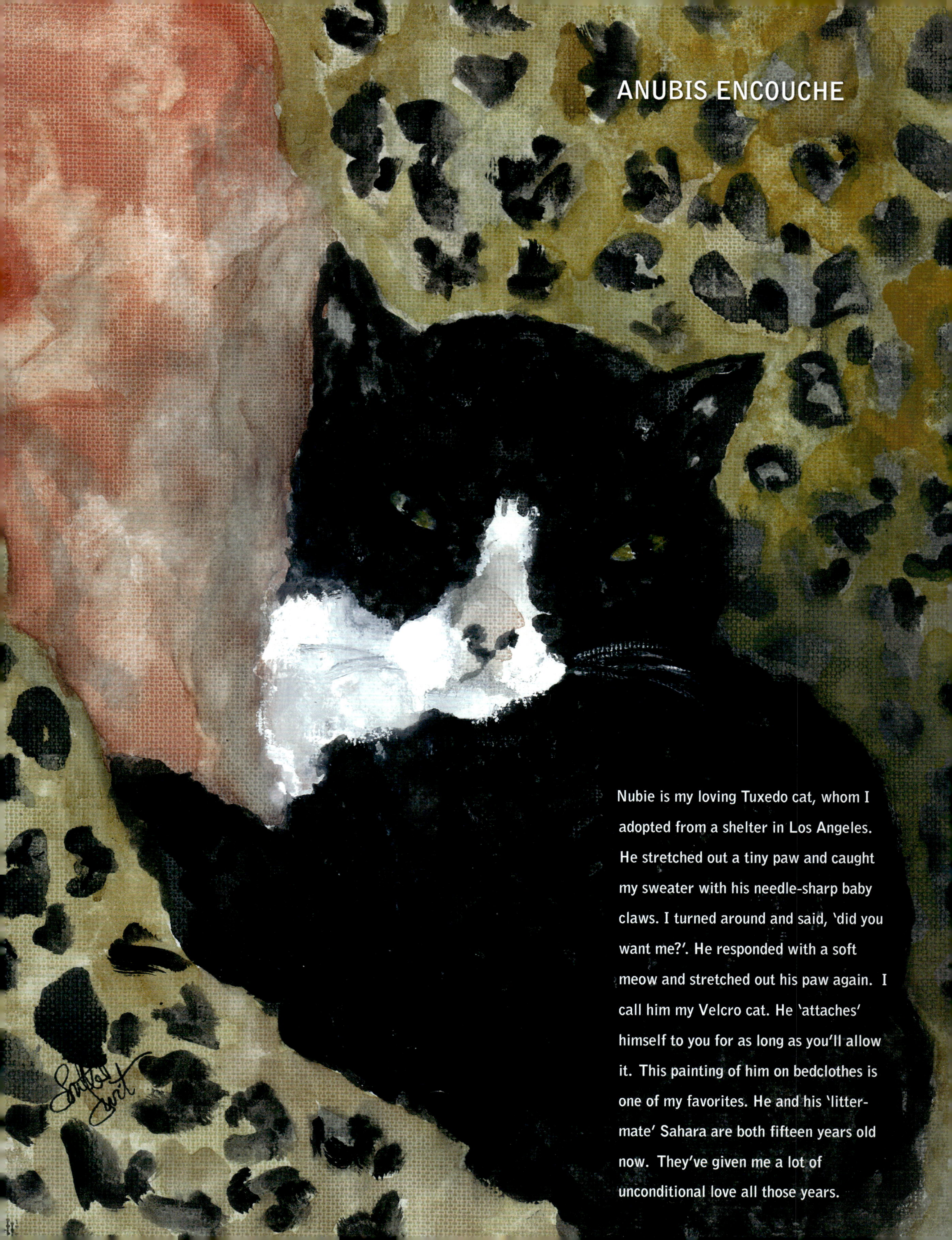

ANUBIS ENCOUCHE

Nubie is my loving Tuxedo cat, whom I adopted from a shelter in Los Angeles. He stretched out a tiny paw and caught my sweater with his needle-sharp baby claws. I turned around and said, 'did you want me?'. He responded with a soft meow and stretched out his paw again. I call him my Velcro cat. He 'attaches' himself to you for as long as you'll allow it. This painting of him on bedclothes is one of my favorites. He and his 'litter-mate' Sahara are both fifteen years old now. They've given me a lot of unconditional love all those years.

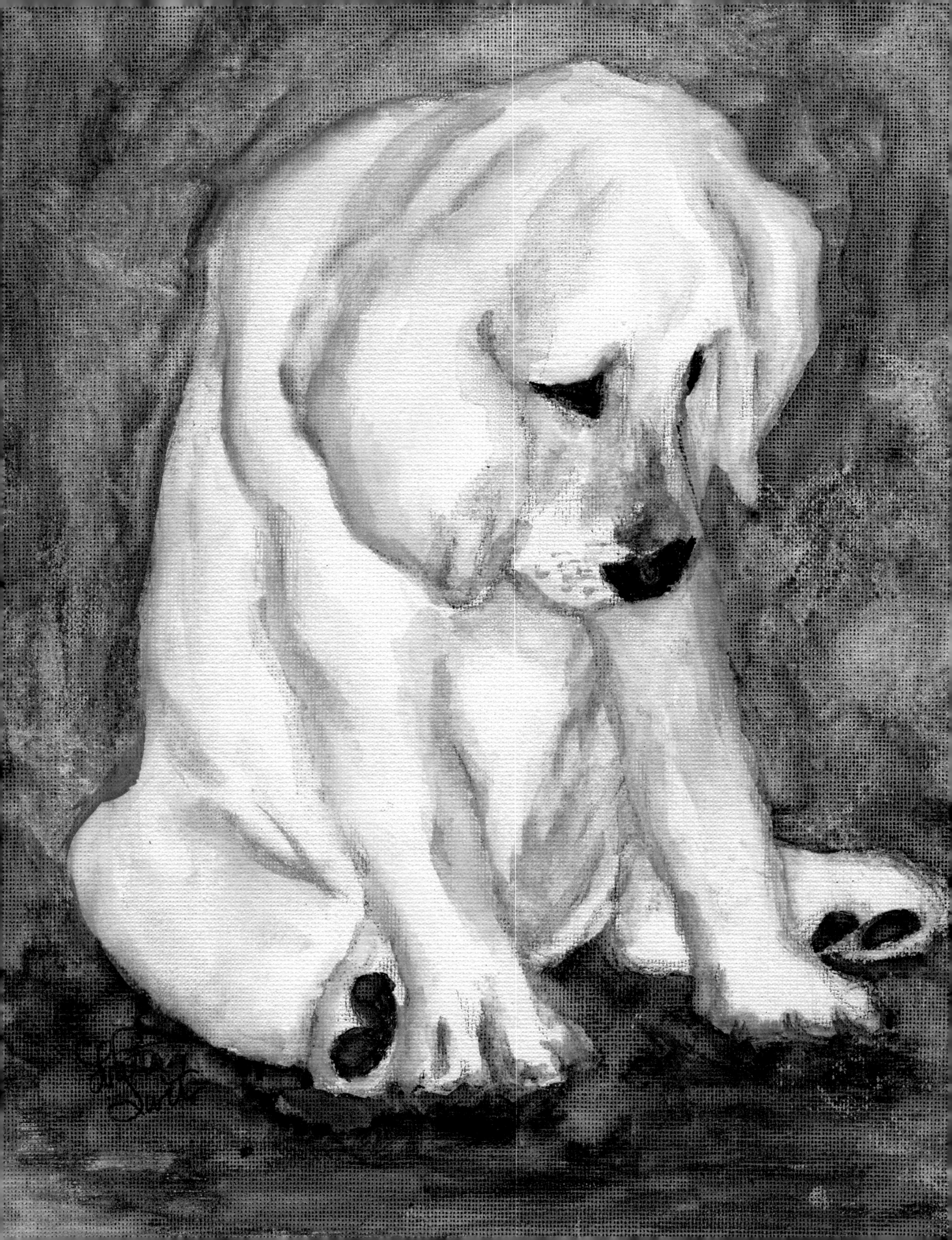

ROOKIE

This Lab puppy was waiting to be evaluated to qualify for training as a Search Dog Rescuer. I was so moved by the photo. Here is this sweet little rescued puppy — anxious, nervous. Will he pass the tests? These dogs, with their handlers, are trained to enter crisis areas to search and rescue survivors. That's right. We rescue them, they rescue us.

It's a win-win situation. The SEARCH DOG FOUNDATION training center is located in Santa Paula, California. They touch my heart, unfailingly. Their courage, intelligence, instinct, and devotion pull at my heartstrings. I've watched them train. It's inspiring. In crisis, it's life-saving.

MONTANA

Big, bold, beautiful Montana lived out his life at the WILDLIFE WAYSTATION. He became so friendly and docile, that with proper handlers, he would attend fund-raisers with us. Rescues at the Waystation have some startling biographies. Reisha, a lion, was rescued guarding a crack house. Just recently, thirteen big cats came to the Waystation from New Zealand, where a zoo had gone bankrupt. On another occasion, we were called in to collect a panther whose cage was being used to smuggle drugs. It's been quite an eventful life for my friend, Martine Collette, who founded the large facility forty years ago. During those years, she rescued more than 77,000 animals. That's not a typo – she was an amazing woman.

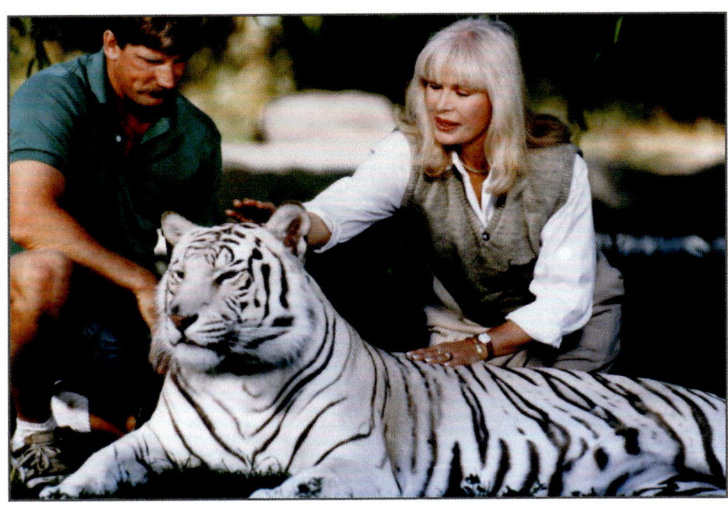

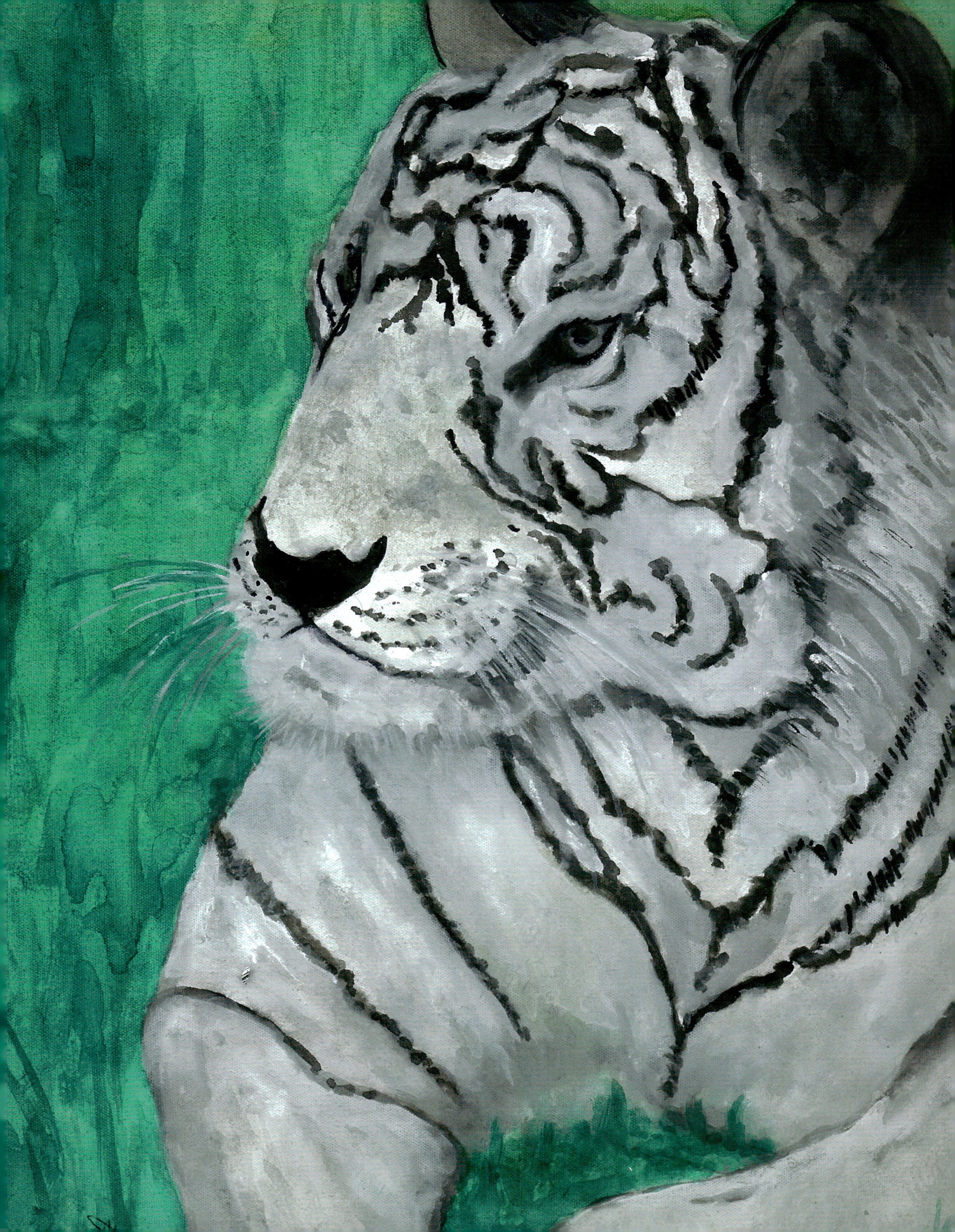

WHITE ROSES

I always think of these roses as the flowers of 'negative space.' I mentioned to a friend of mine that I was planning to experiment with painting a bowl of white roses. 'Ah,' she said knowingly, 'you'll be using negative space.'

'Say what?' I thought. The truth is, it can be wonderful not knowing technically what you're doing. It's liberating! You don't know what you don't know. It gives you great freedom; you make mistakes, which is great. If you don't make mistakes, how can you learn? How will you know how good you can be?

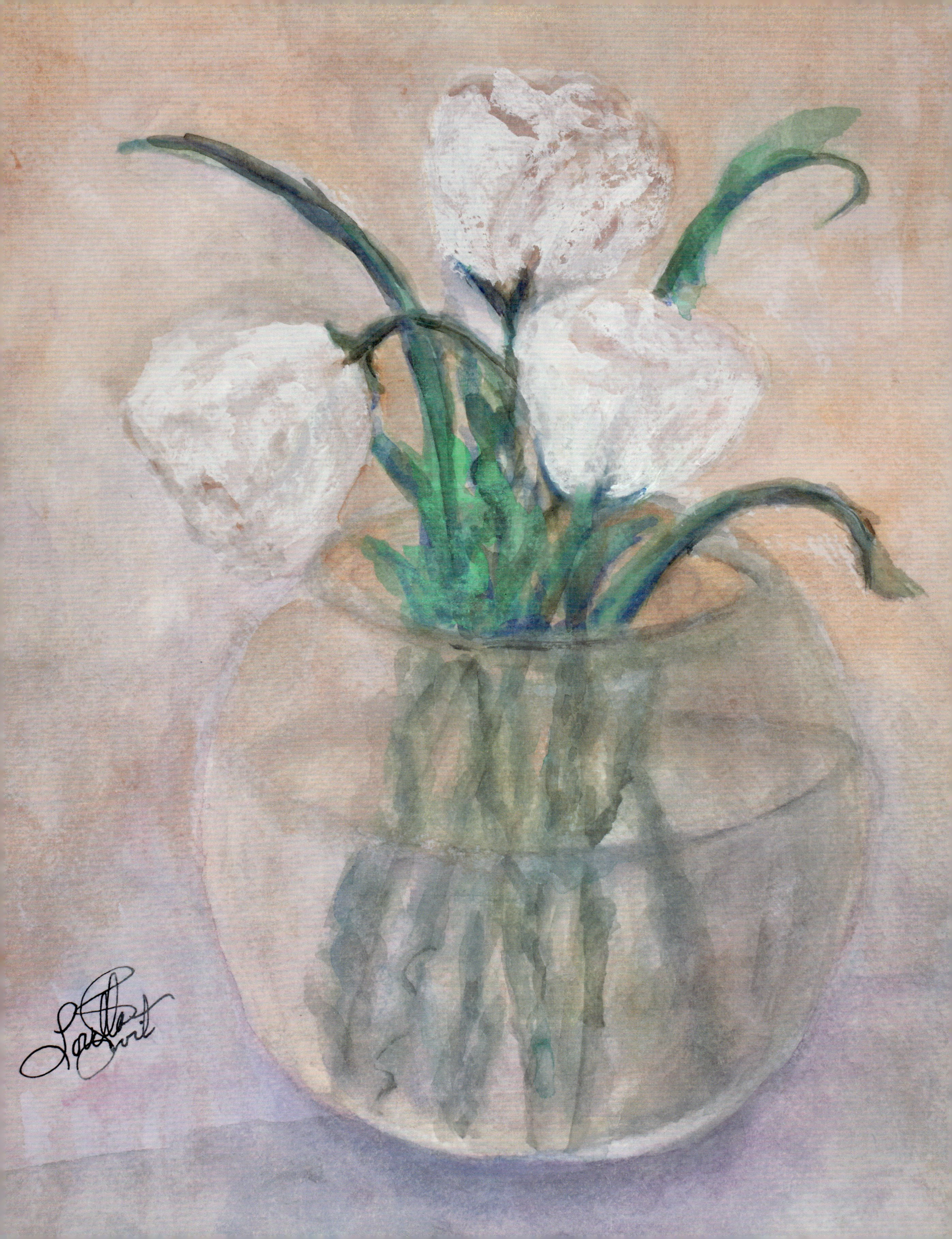

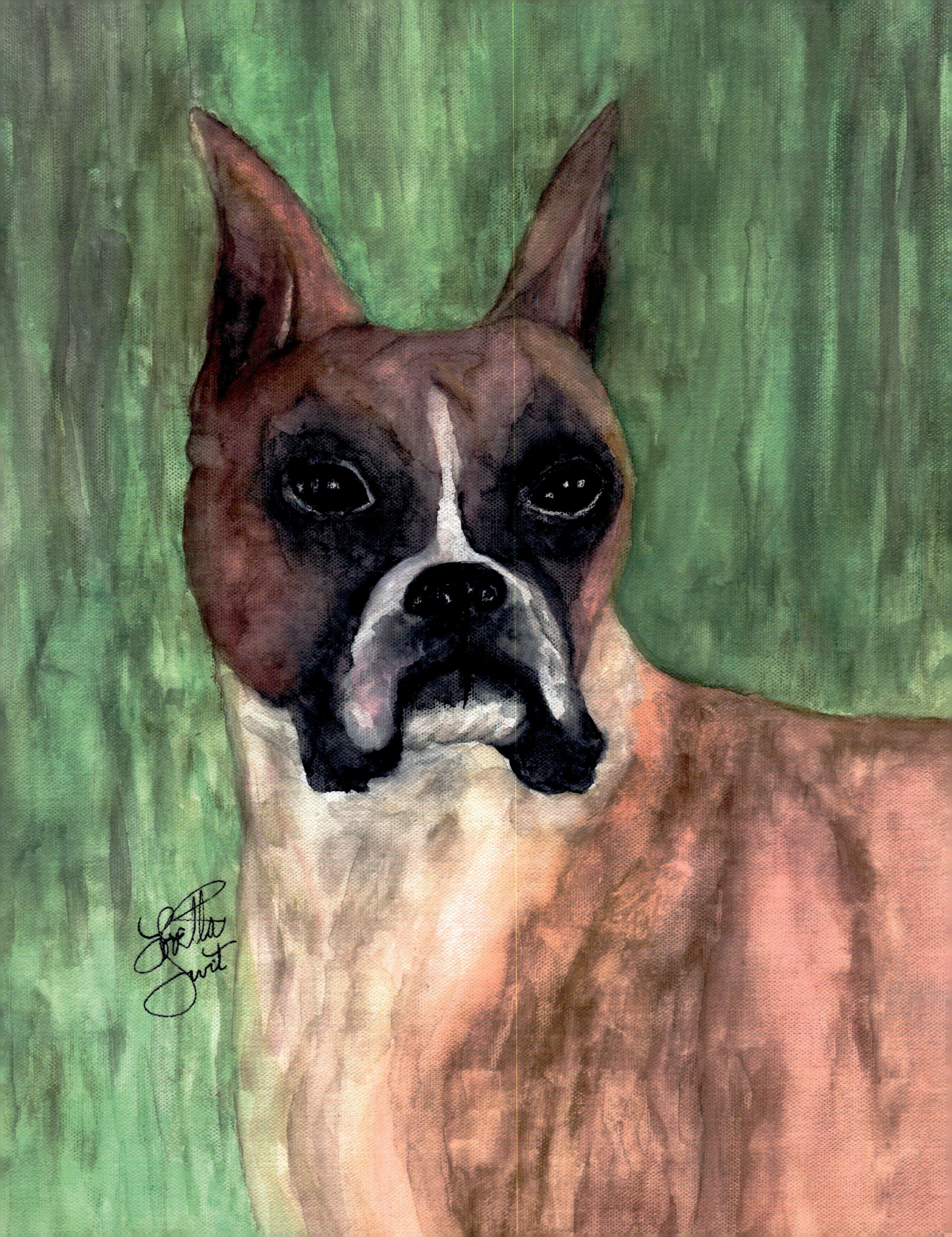

PRINCE

I found my handsome "Prince" in a calendar. He is so elegant. I decided to try and paint my first Boxer. The markings are interesting. The ears, always at attention, as his very presence commands. I've had friends and associates over the years who have an absolute allegiance to the breed.

ACTORS AND OTHERS FOR ANIMALS, where I am privileged to serve as 1st Vice President, is headed by President JoAnne Worley. With a dedicated, impassioned Board, we speak for those who cannot speak for themselves.

Sometimes we shout and roar!

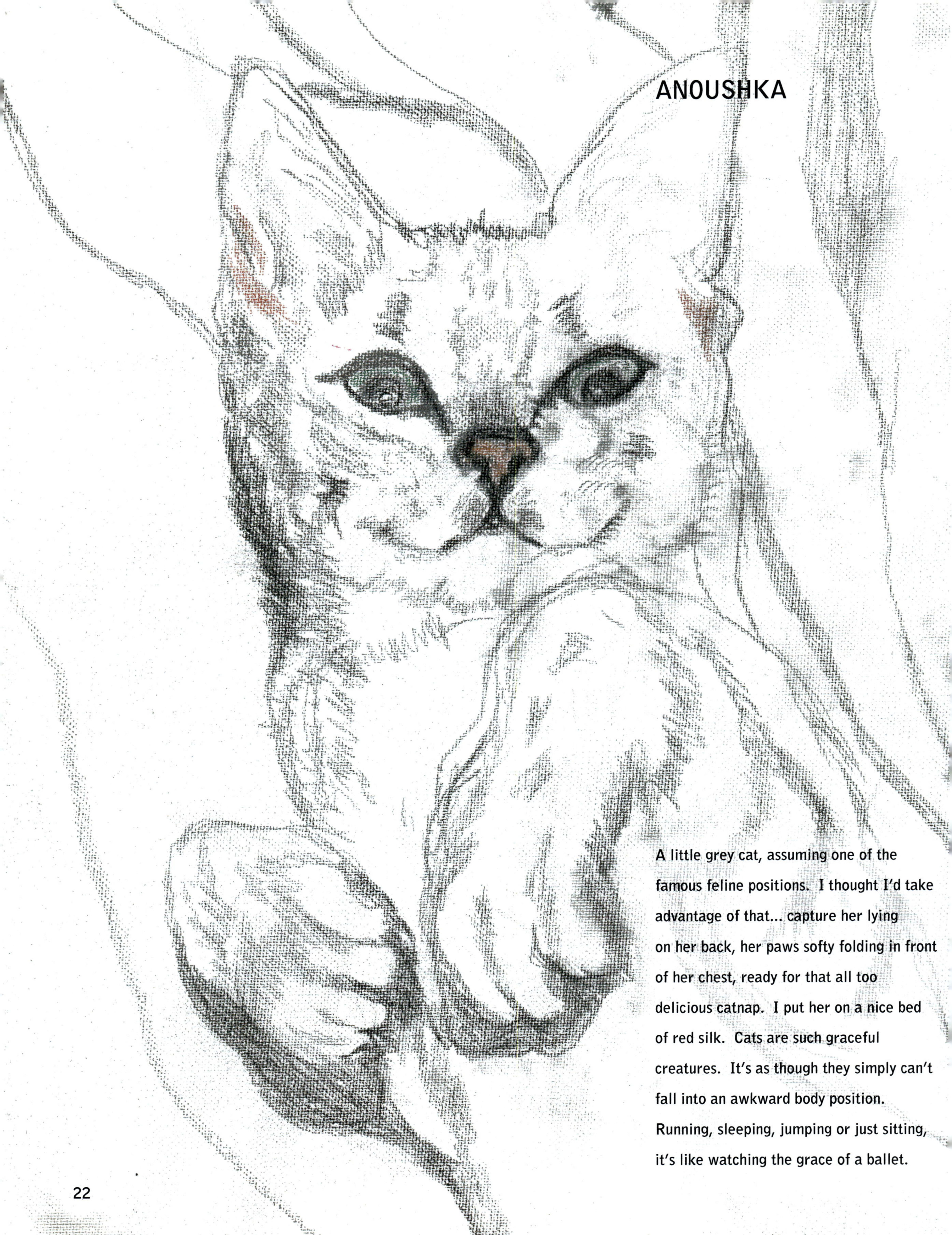

ANOUSHKA

A little grey cat, assuming one of the famous feline positions. I thought I'd take advantage of that... capture her lying on her back, her paws softy folding in front of her chest, ready for that all too delicious catnap. I put her on a nice bed of red silk. Cats are such graceful creatures. It's as though they simply can't fall into an awkward body position. Running, sleeping, jumping or just sitting, it's like watching the grace of a ballet.

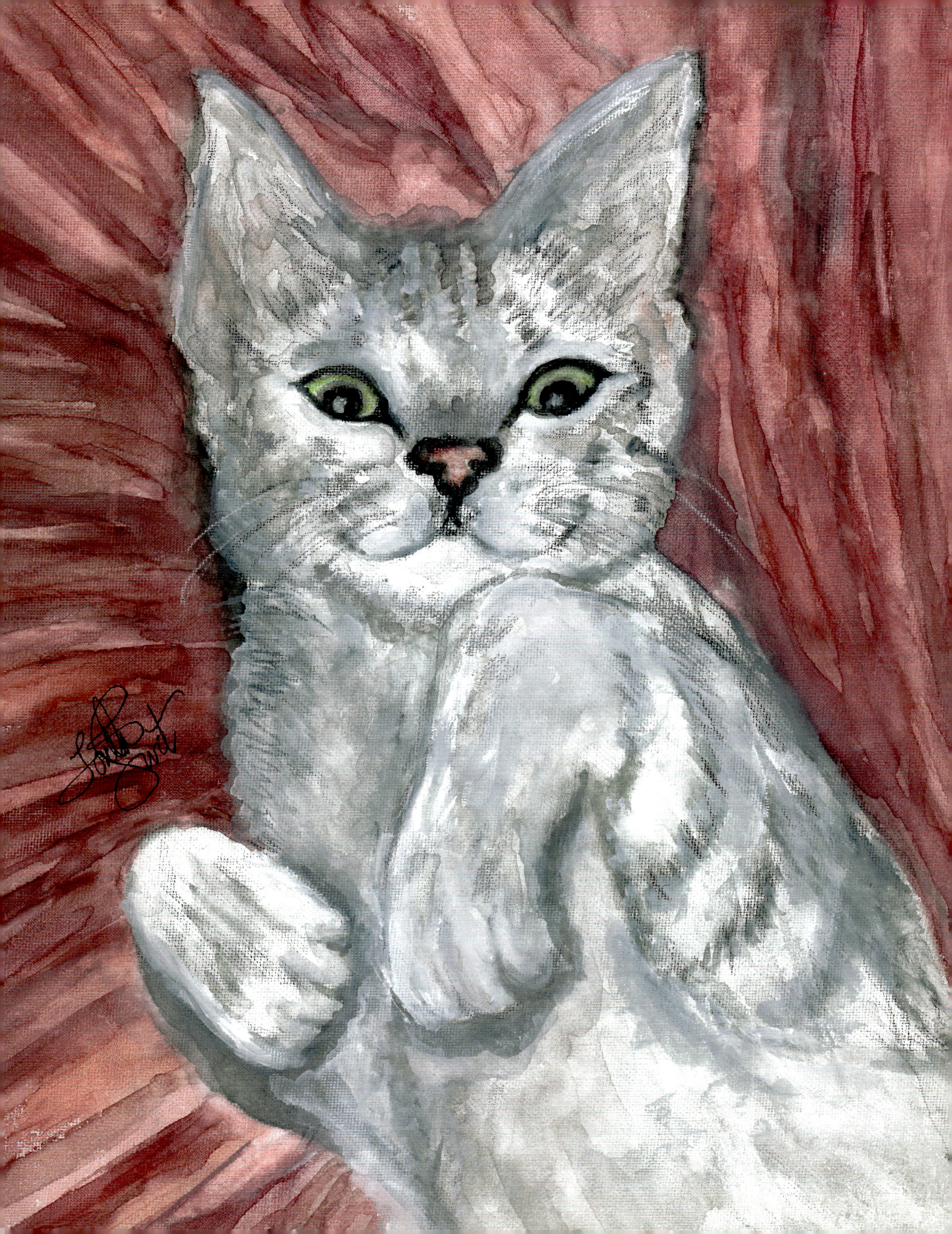

ISIS IN THE ROSEBUSHES

ISIS was one of my own cats......... or was I one of her humans? A member of her staff, perhaps? Catlovers will understand that. ISIS was a goddess in her manner. Not overly social, but if you were on the receiving end of a lick and a purr, it was close to a sanctification. When I adopted her, she looked like a tiny white mouse. As she matured, she blossomed into one gorgeous feline with the thick, beautiful coat of a Turkish Angora. She was a study in pastels, all pink and white and creamy. My friends have called it my Monet moment.

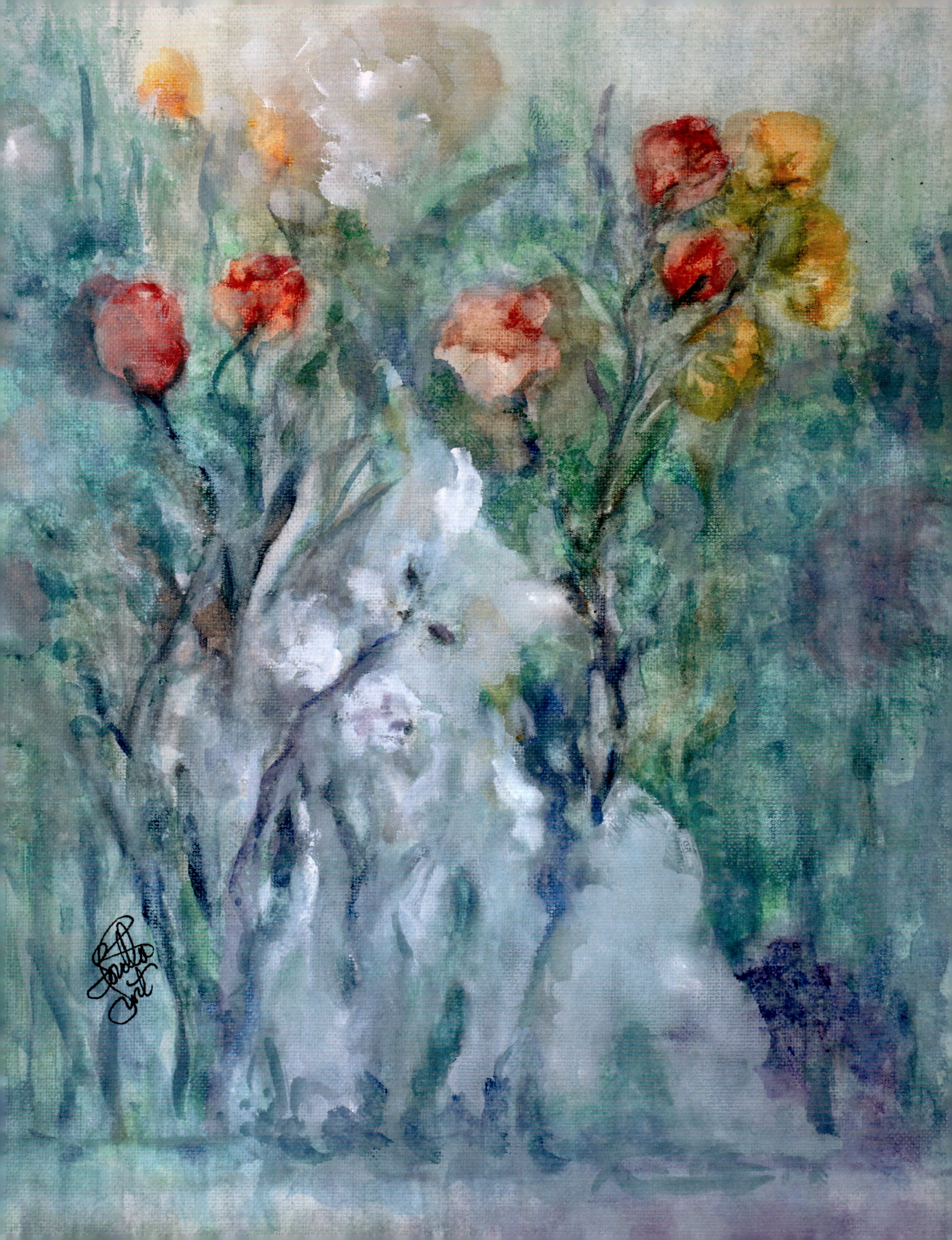

HAPPY DAY

I am unapologetic about being crazy for goats. I find them to be the cutest, funniest, dearest comedians on the planet. They're pushy, sweet and just plain adorable.

I most love the texture of Happy Day's horns. He lives a happy life at the FARM SANCTUARY, an organization co-founded by Gene Baur, a relentless activist who has achieved monumental success in bringing about more compassionate, humane conditions for farm animals. He's an extraordinary man who walks the talk in his unending quest to end cruelty.

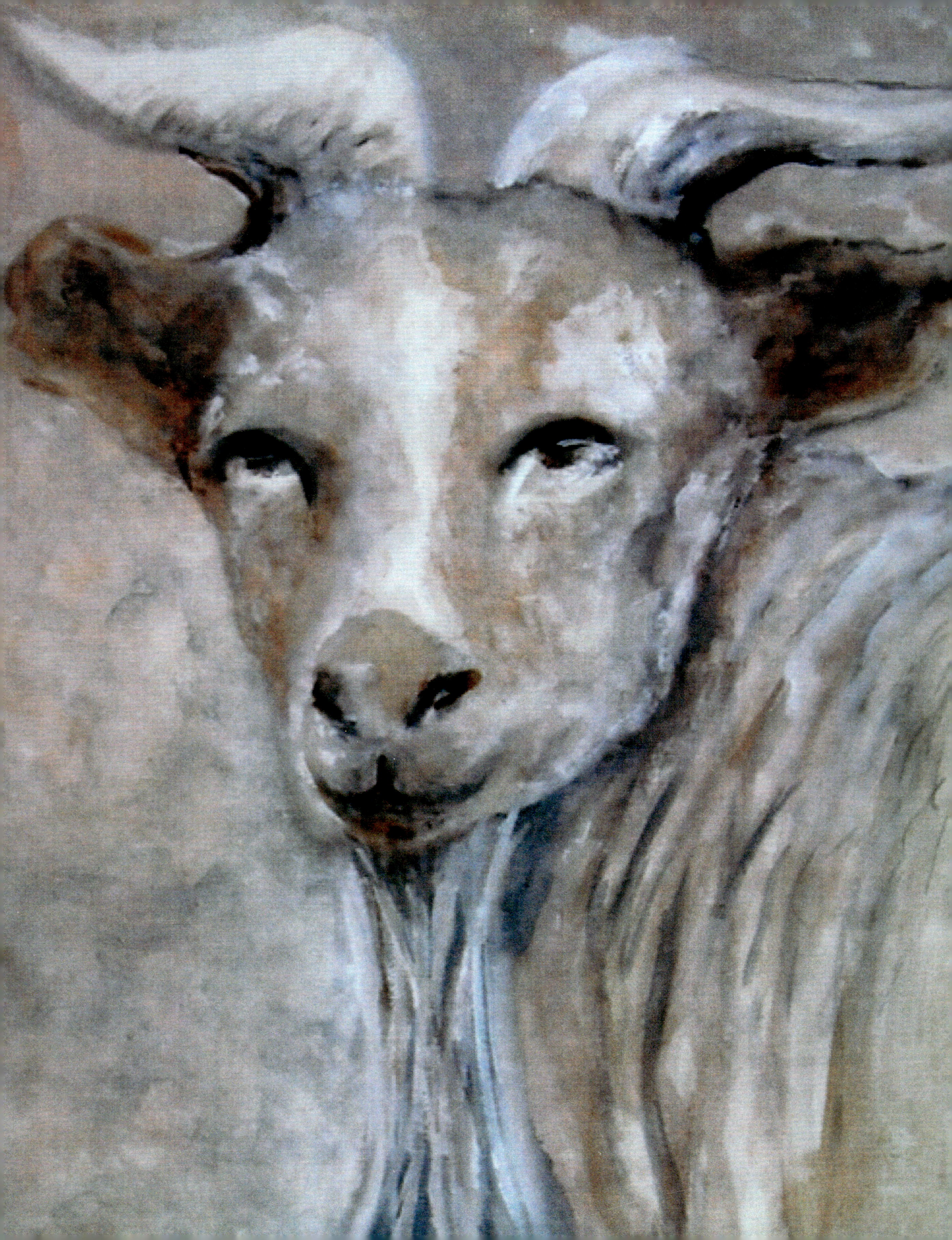

PURPLE IRIS

I had been focusing on my animal art for so long a time that I all but forgot this sweet Iris painting. I'm glad it resurfaced to be included here. I enjoy painting florals, even a few landscapes, but my animal portraiture brings my artwork full circle with my activism. Many animal portraits I've done were difficult for me, but by the last brushstroke, I became better able to tackle the next challenge.

It was such a strange experience to stand back and re-evaluate Purple Iris, seeing it as though I were a stranger. I found myself smiling and liking it!

Hope springs eternal.

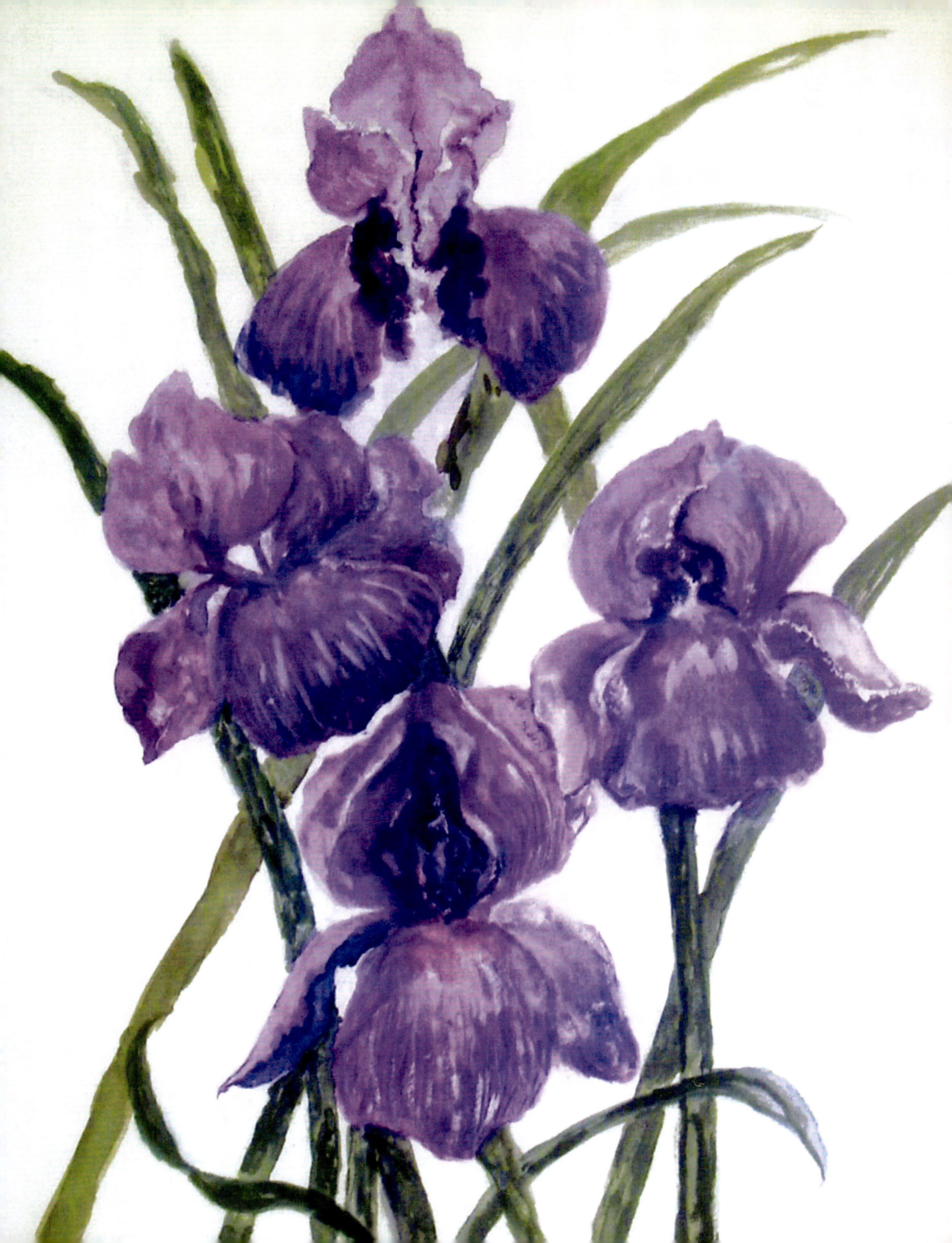

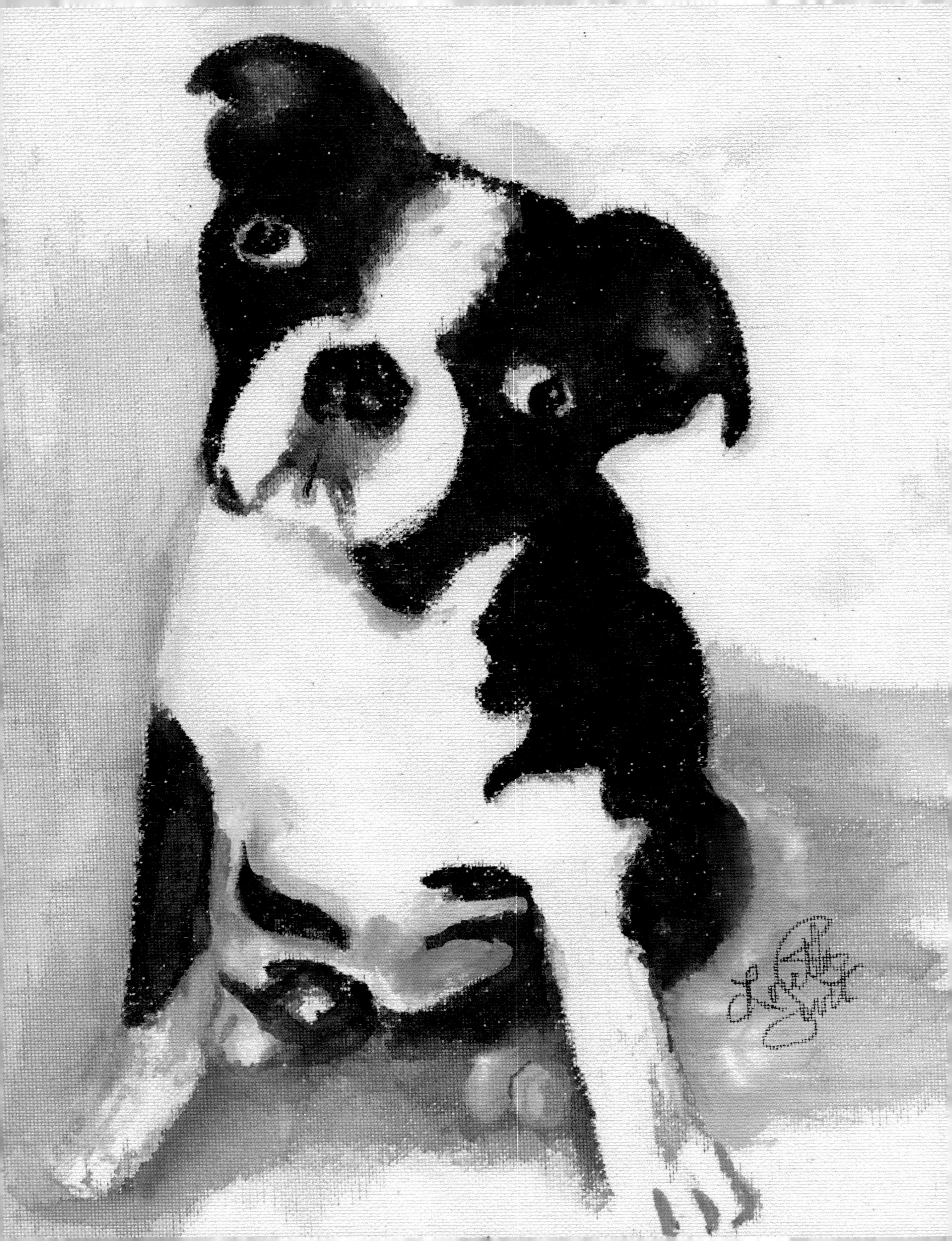

LOVEY

This Boston Terrier came to me in the form of a greeting card containing a charming, funny note from a group of nurses who were in the audience one night at a performance of 'Move Over Mrs. Markham,' a wonderful farce I was playing in at the New Theatre.

As you may know, the traditional wish for good luck is to say, 'Break a leg' to the performer. The note read that I could break my leg. There were nurses in the audience who would be able to set it and care for me. I met with them afterwards, and we had a good laugh.

I painted the Boston Baby and gave the original to the director. He had just rescued a Boston Terrier who looked exactly like the painting. He had a herd of rescues, a very caring man, not to mention the fabulous job he had done directing the play.

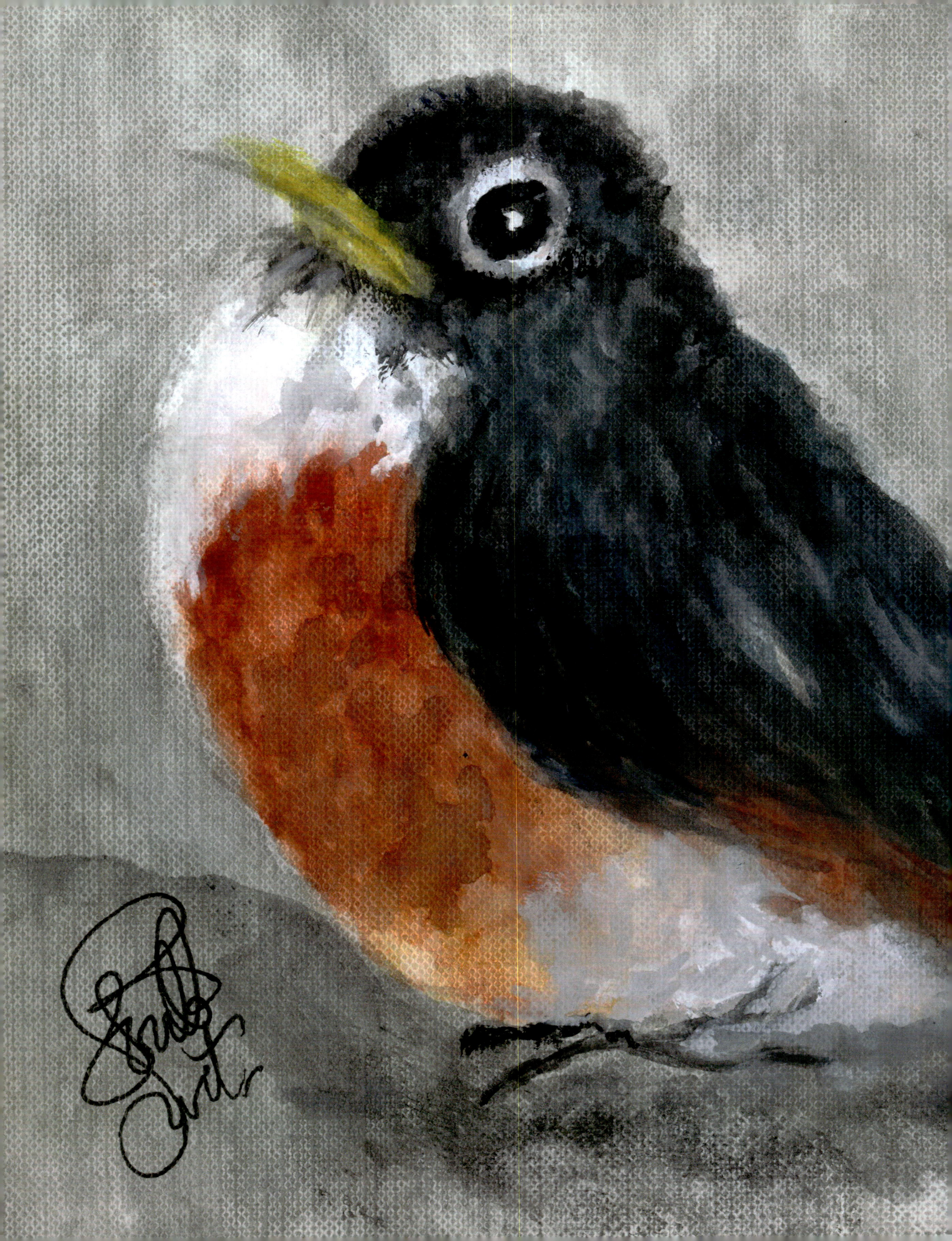

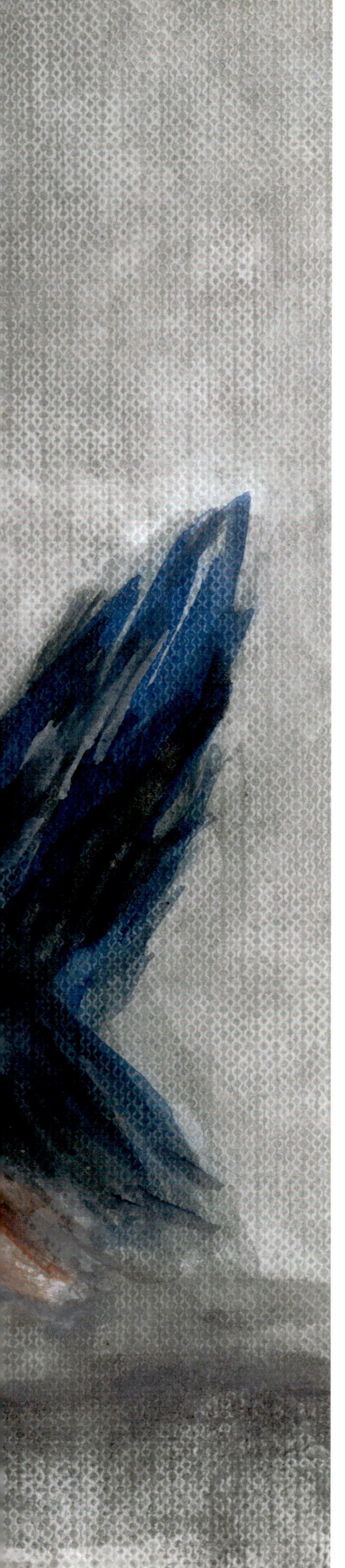

A ROBIN IN PARIS

I was staying in a friend's delightful apartment in Paris. I was loafing on the balcony, leafing through a magazine, when I saw a photo of this little Robin. Turned out loafing and leafing through pages was more rewarding than expected. I began doodling and soon gave way to full-out paints and brushes.

I frame this sweet little in a gallery that resembled a movie set from a French film noir. You can always rely on Paris for atmosphere. It was such a lovely little painting. So much so that it was stolen at an art show in Malibu. What goes around comes around. Be sorry for them. C'est la vie.

GOLDEN IN SHADOWS

My friends call this my 'Rembrandt' moment – all dark and brown and in shadow. They dubbed 'Isis in the Rosebushes' (page 25, my gentle Monet moment. With great artists like those for inspiration, and friends like those for support, it's little wonder I continue to paint so fearlessly. This beautiful Search Rescue retriever was my 'Golden' inspiration.

The photo is worth a thousand words. The painting, I hope, speaks for itself.

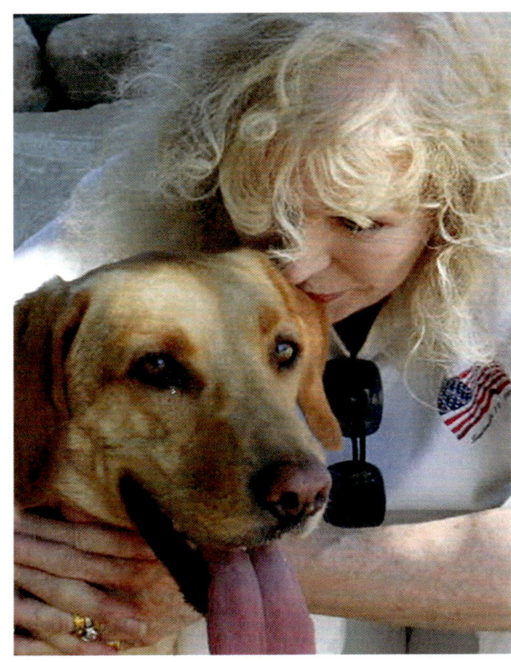

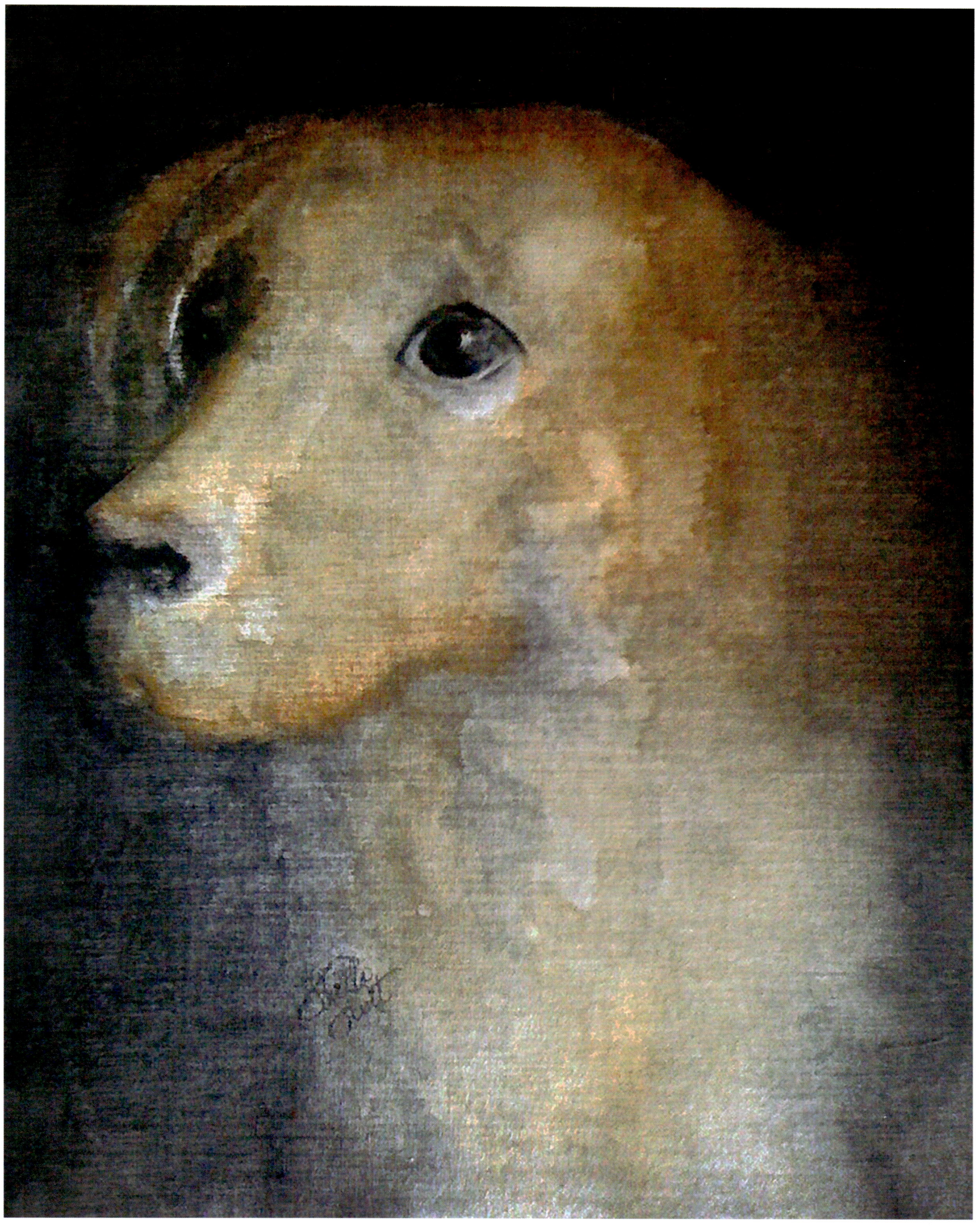

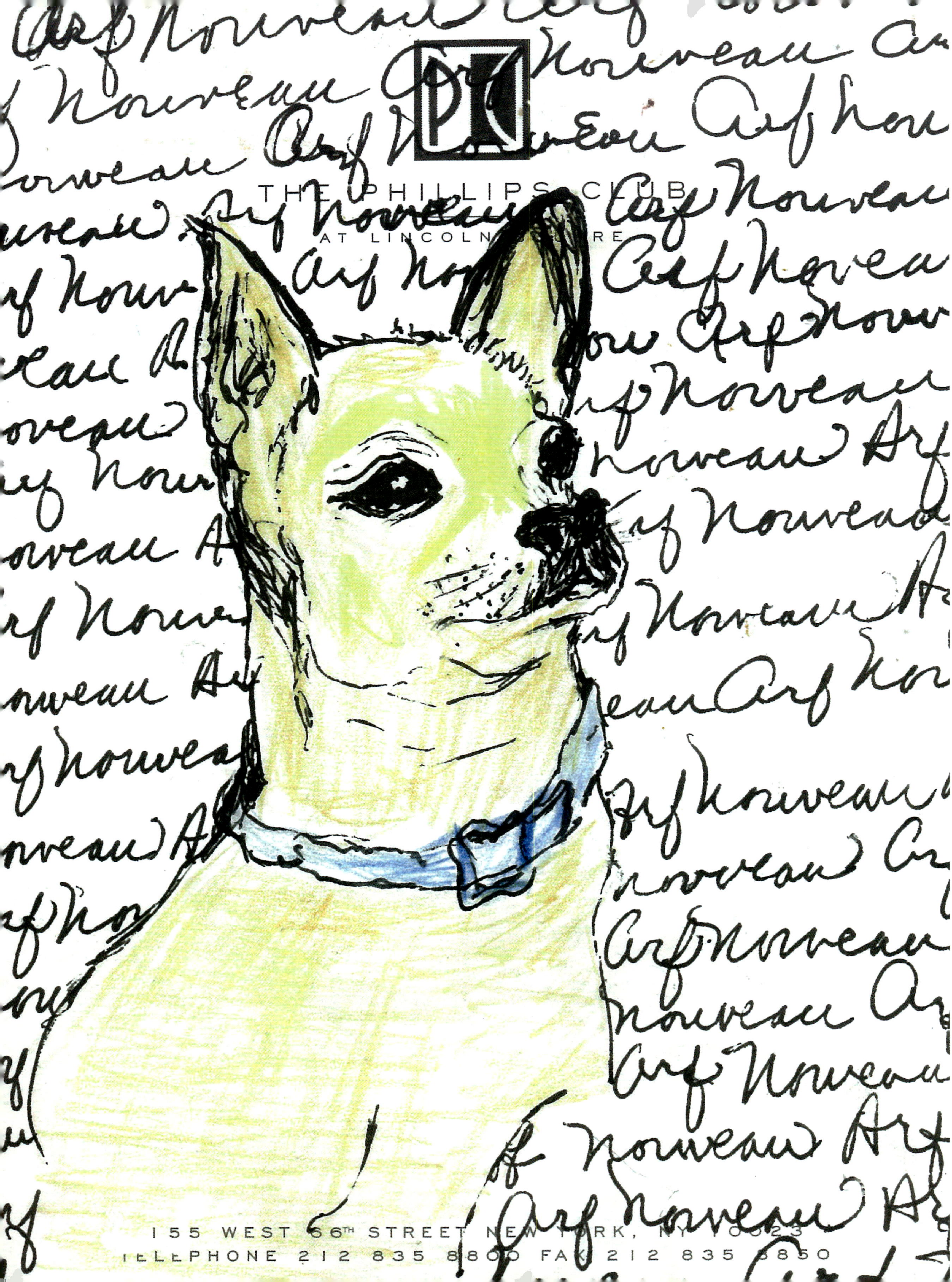

PC

THE PHILLIPS CLUB
AT LINCOLN SQUARE

Arf Nouveau

155 WEST 66TH STREET NEW YORK, NY 10023
TELEPHONE 212 835 8800 FAX 212 835 8850

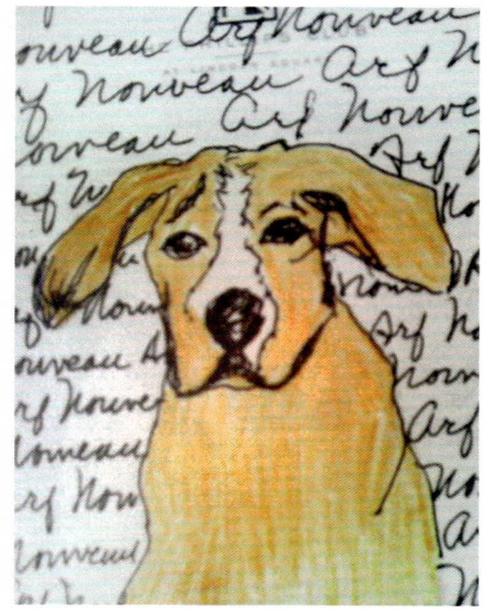

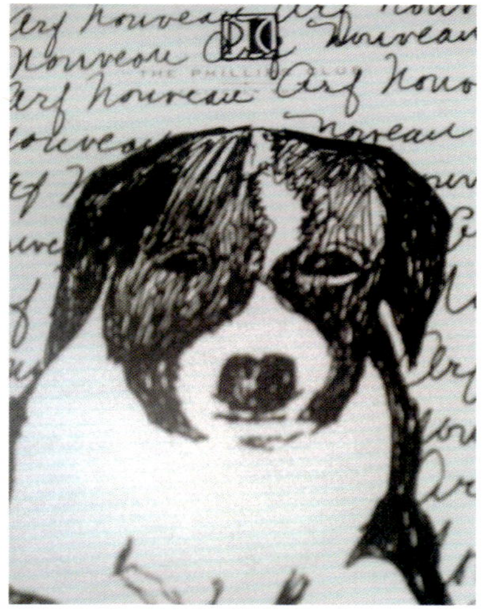

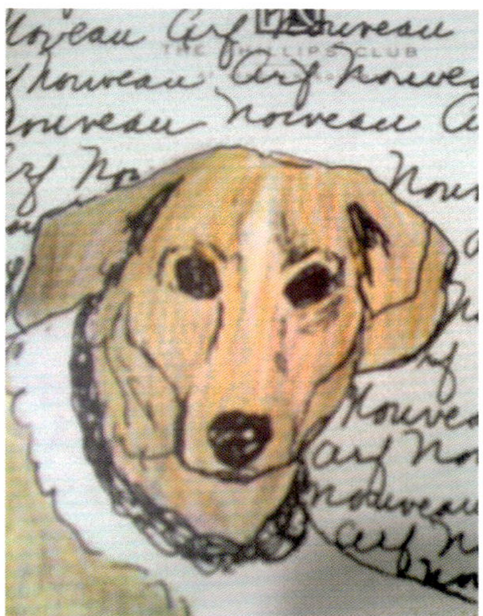

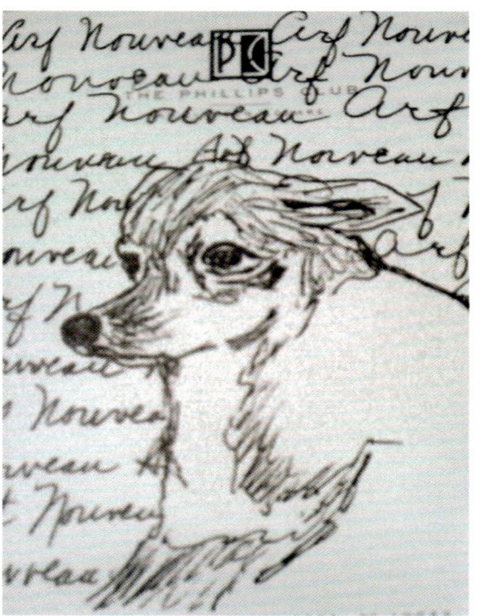

DOODLING FOR FUN & AUCTION

So many good ideas can sprout from doodling. I can't help myself. It's an addiction. I've been jokingly referred to as a serial doodler. These sketches began as a collection in one small tablet for auction at one of my fund-raisers. I thought it might be something a collector/animal lover would enjoy. We'll call it 'Sketchels by Swit'........ why not? It would be fun. It's on my 'to do' list, and my friends all know I can't help myself.

FREE

The blaze on his forehead resembled that of my first horse, Mr. TenMan. "Free" is much younger and has a wild freedom about him that "Ten" didn't have. The bonding that occurs when your discipline is Hunter/Jumpers is practically spiritual. Your horse can feel your eyes look over at the next fence and change leads before you even signal him to do it. It's a very special excitement; one like no other. They have such strength and such beauty. I love washing them, brushing their manes, kissing and stroking their velvet noses.

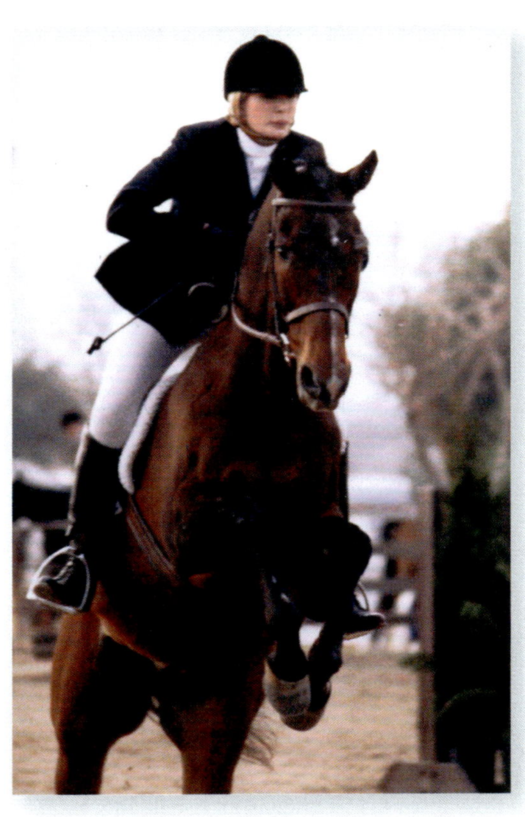

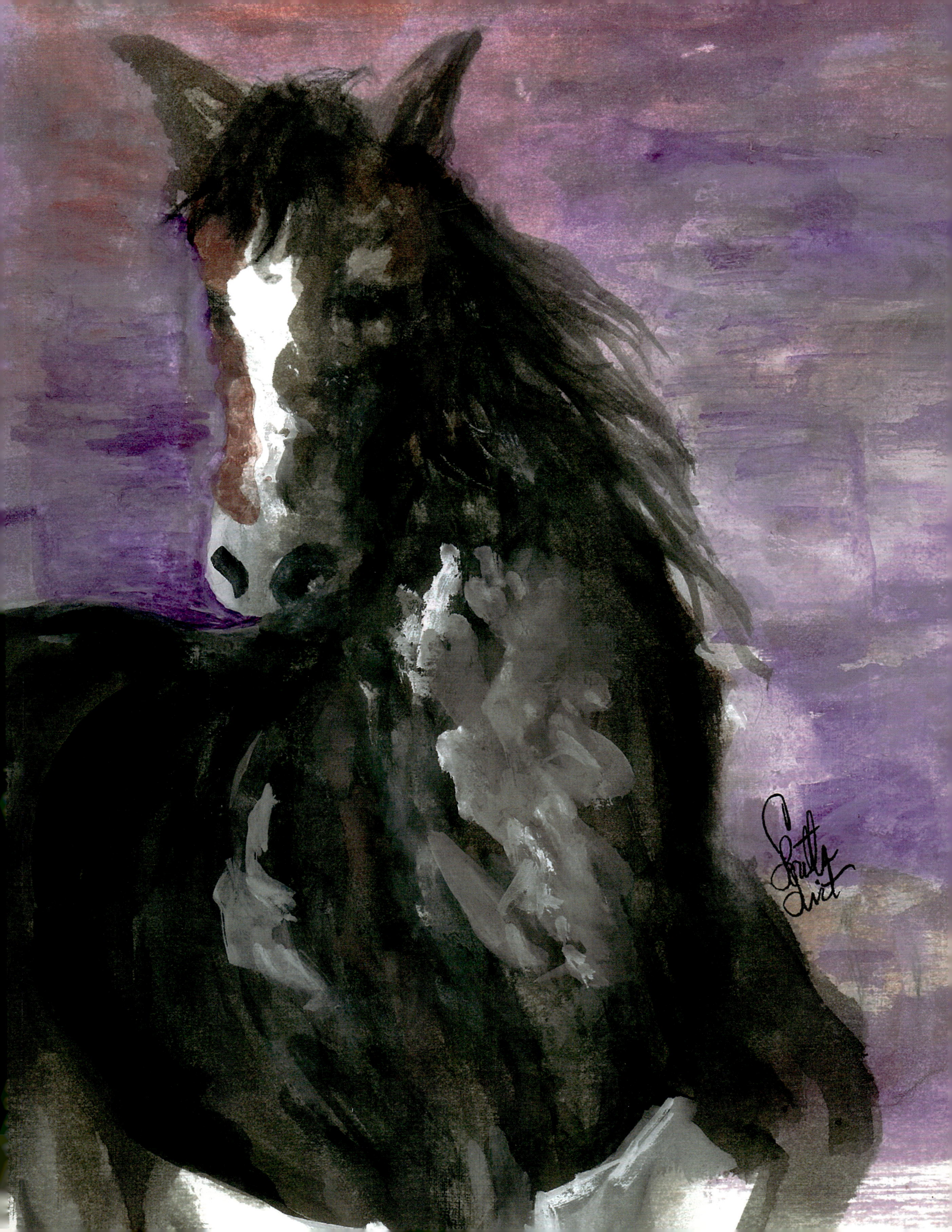

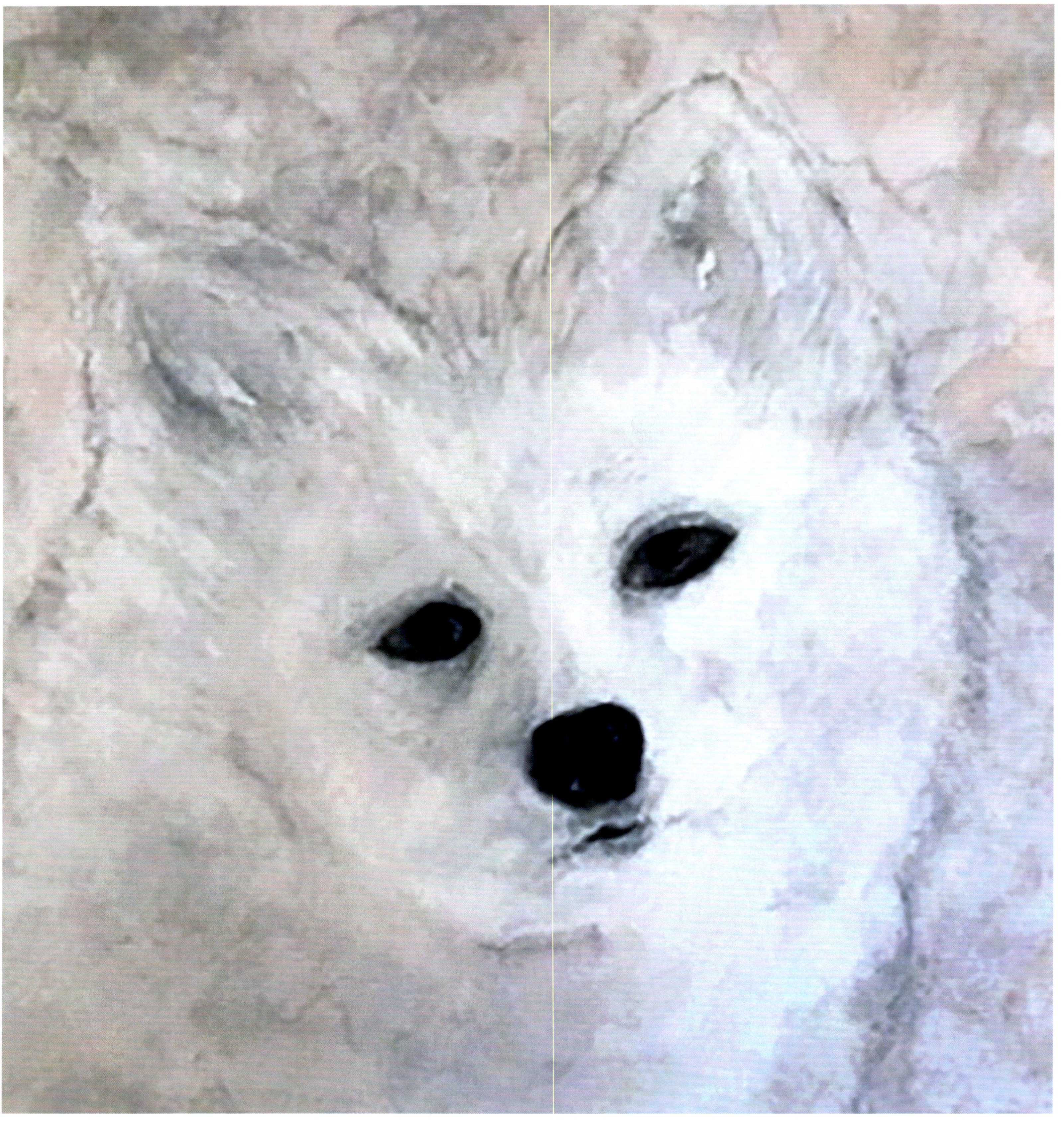

SAMANTHA

I was approached to paint beloved Samantha after she had passed on. The idea was to try to achieve a heavenly environment for her in the painting. I wanted a serene, dreamy quality to engulf her on the canvas, to let her light-colored fur blend into the clouds as if she were floating softly in heaven.

It's a belief that all our animal companions are up there waiting for us — young, happy and healthy, waiting to jump all over us, the way they did on earth when we would come home. I'd like to believe that......... it's such a heavenly thought!

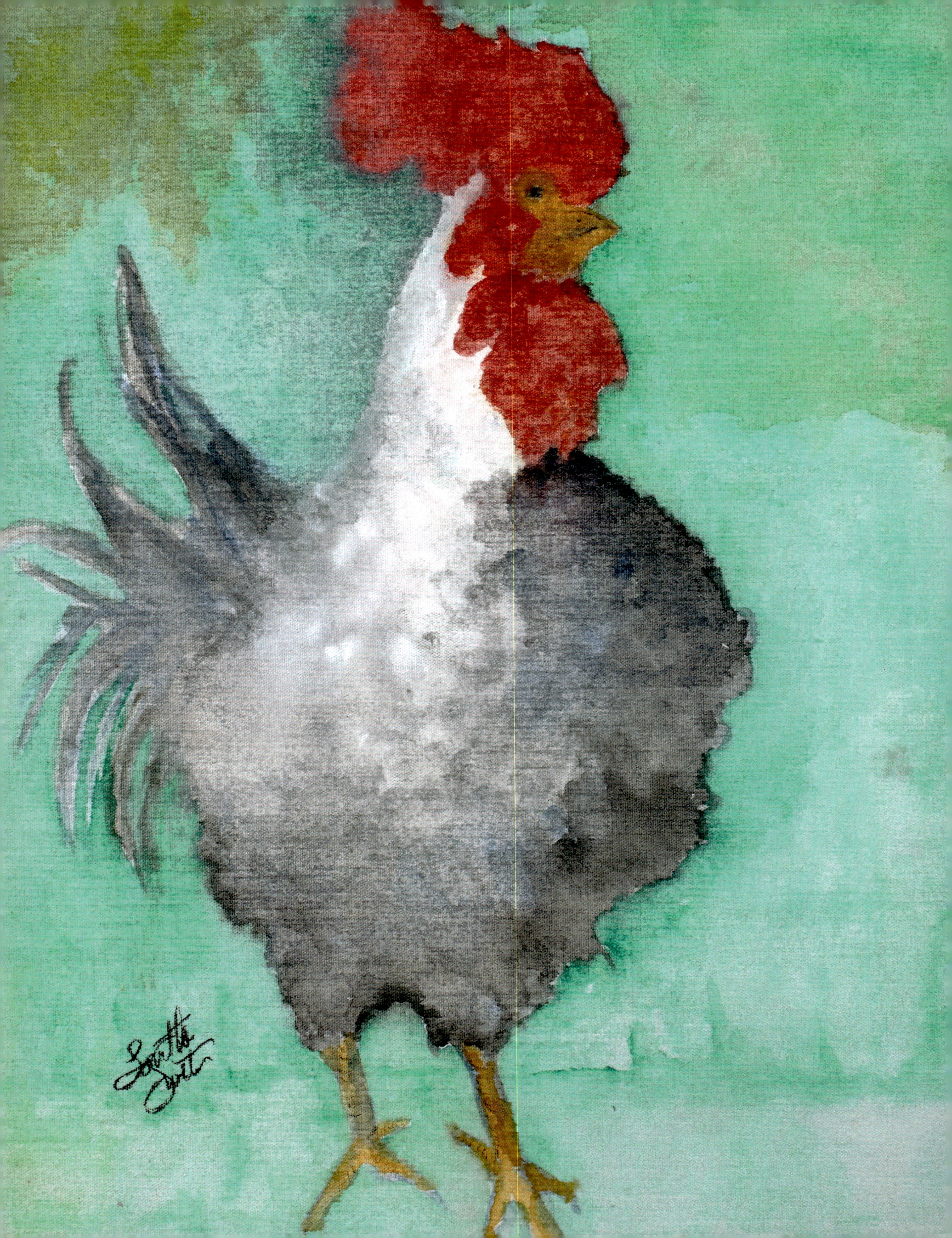

CHUTZPAH

He could have no other name... Chutzpah! Such élan! Such pluck! Gumption, that's what. He holds a special place in my heart and on my kitchen wall.

Using that vibrant background was very different for me. I want always for my subject to outshine everything else, but this rooster was so strong, he dazzled hotter than any color I could choose. I picture him running things in the barnyard......... totally in charge and keeping everything in order!

Quel esprit!

AUGIE-DOGGIE

Her name was Augusta, named after the famous golf course in Georgia. However, the children in the household quickly nicknamed her Augie. When grandchildren arrived on the scene, the name evolved into Augie-Doggie.

Fairly soon, nobody used the elegant name of Augusta any longer – the first-class golf course for which she was named had all but been forgotten.

She remained Augie-Doggie to everyone for the rest of her life.

Personally, I think it suits her.

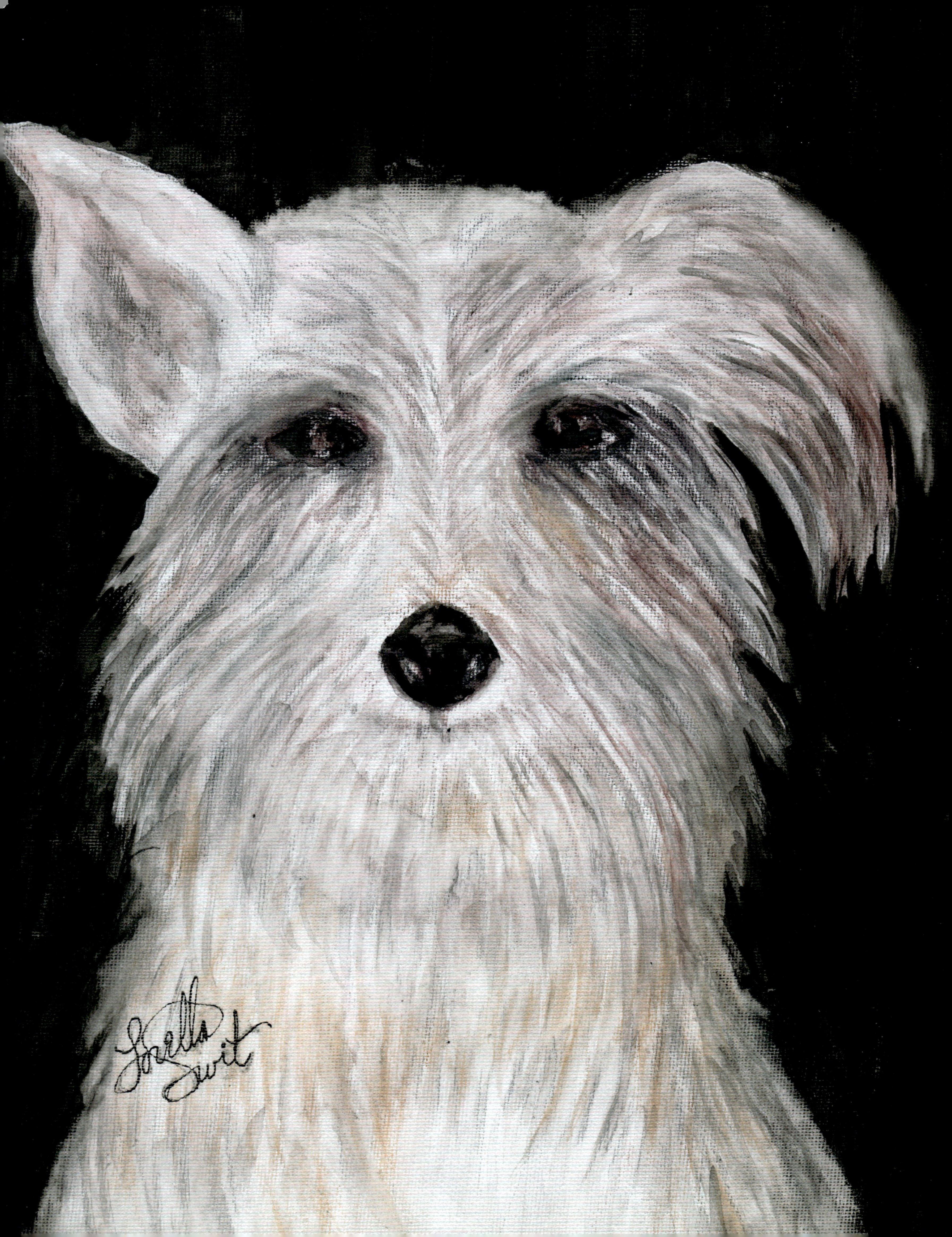
Loretta Swit

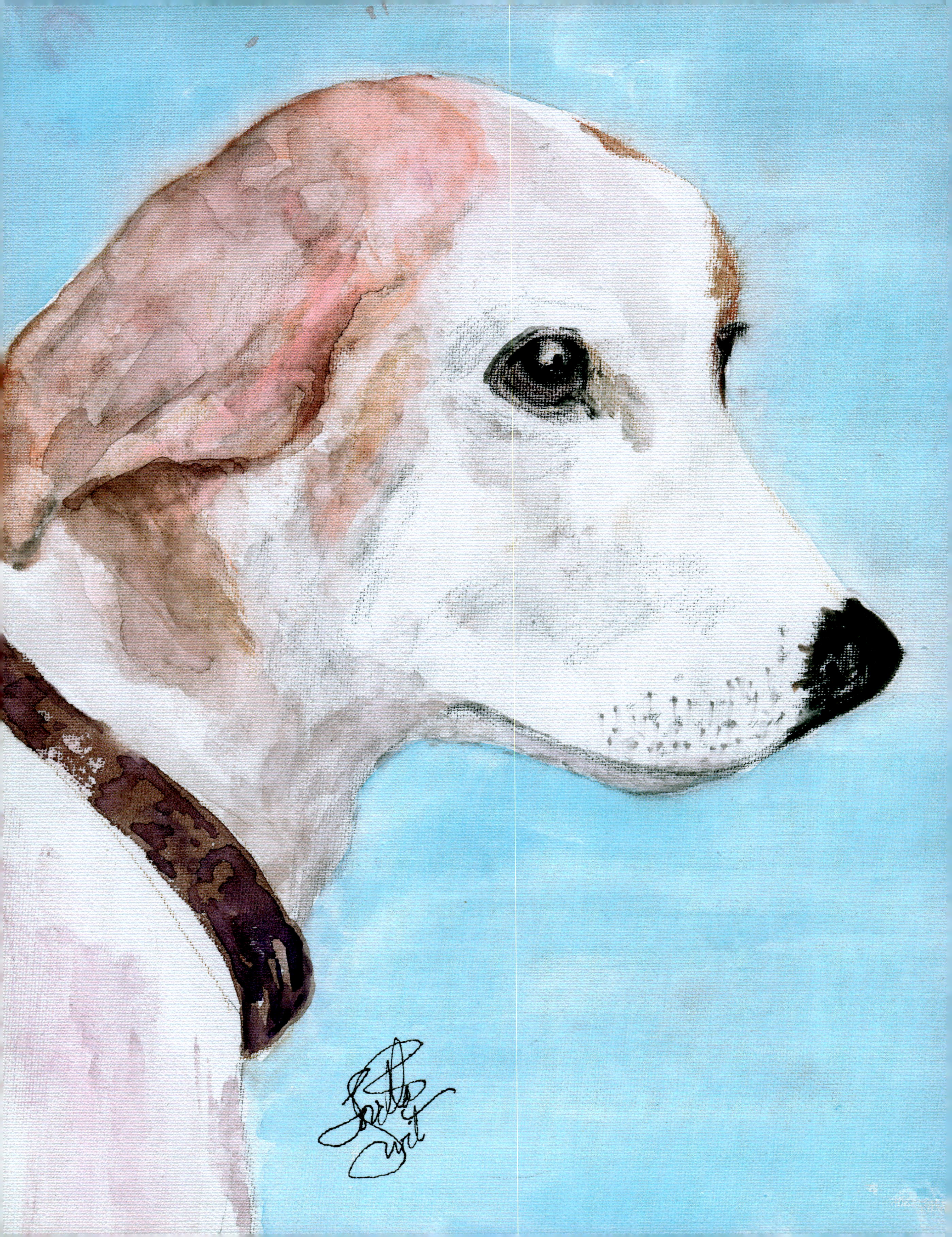

BUDDY

Buddy is almost a study in pastels, which is why I painted his collar a deep color. Buddy decorates the wall at Dogtown , a boarding/grooming facility in St. Augustine. They've attended Ayla's Acres fund-raisers and have bought several paintings of mine for their offices. I'm an Honorary Board member at AYLA'S ACRES NO-KILL ANIMAL RESCUE. We are currently housing about 150 animals, some of which are not adoptable, unless you want to adopt a goat, in which case we'd be delighted to discuss it.

If you find yourself in lovely, quaint St. Augustine, Florida, please drop in to our Ayla's Acres Thrift Shop, managed by Board members and volunteers, the proceeds from the sales go straight to our shelter.

CHAMOISE

Legend would have you believe that the first of the breed was the result of mating a lion cub and a monkey. I had been smitten with the "Butterfly Dogs of Peking" for years. One of mine, Croissant, was a "Sleeve Peke", so-named because the priests in ancient China carried them in their long, voluminous sleeves.

For a brief time, I entered Croissant at dog shows. Inordinately beautiful with her Pansy Flower face, she would glide into the arena, her long silky coat covering any evidence of her paws. She looked as though she were on a skateboard. She was irresistible and usually brought home a blue ribbon and a silver cup.

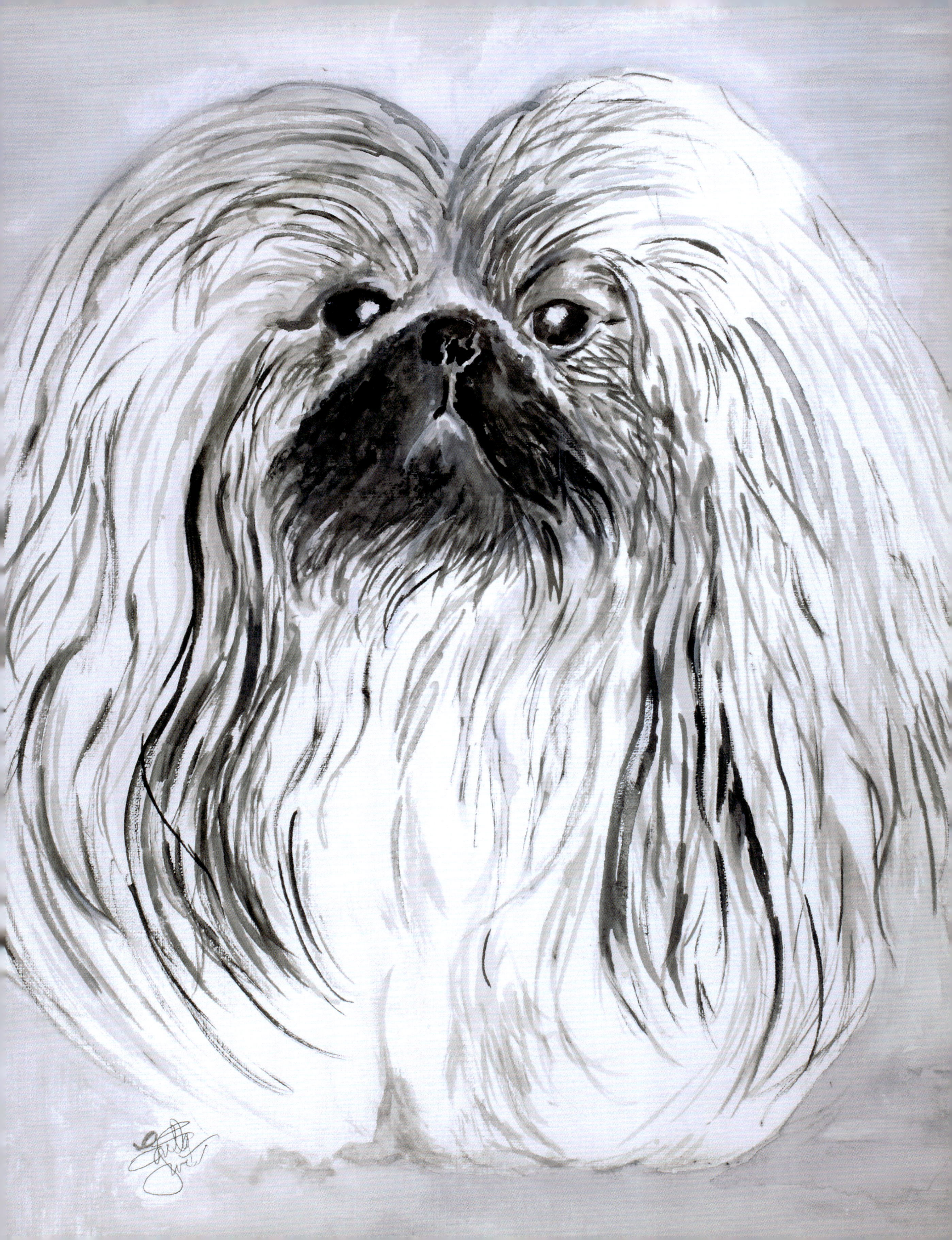

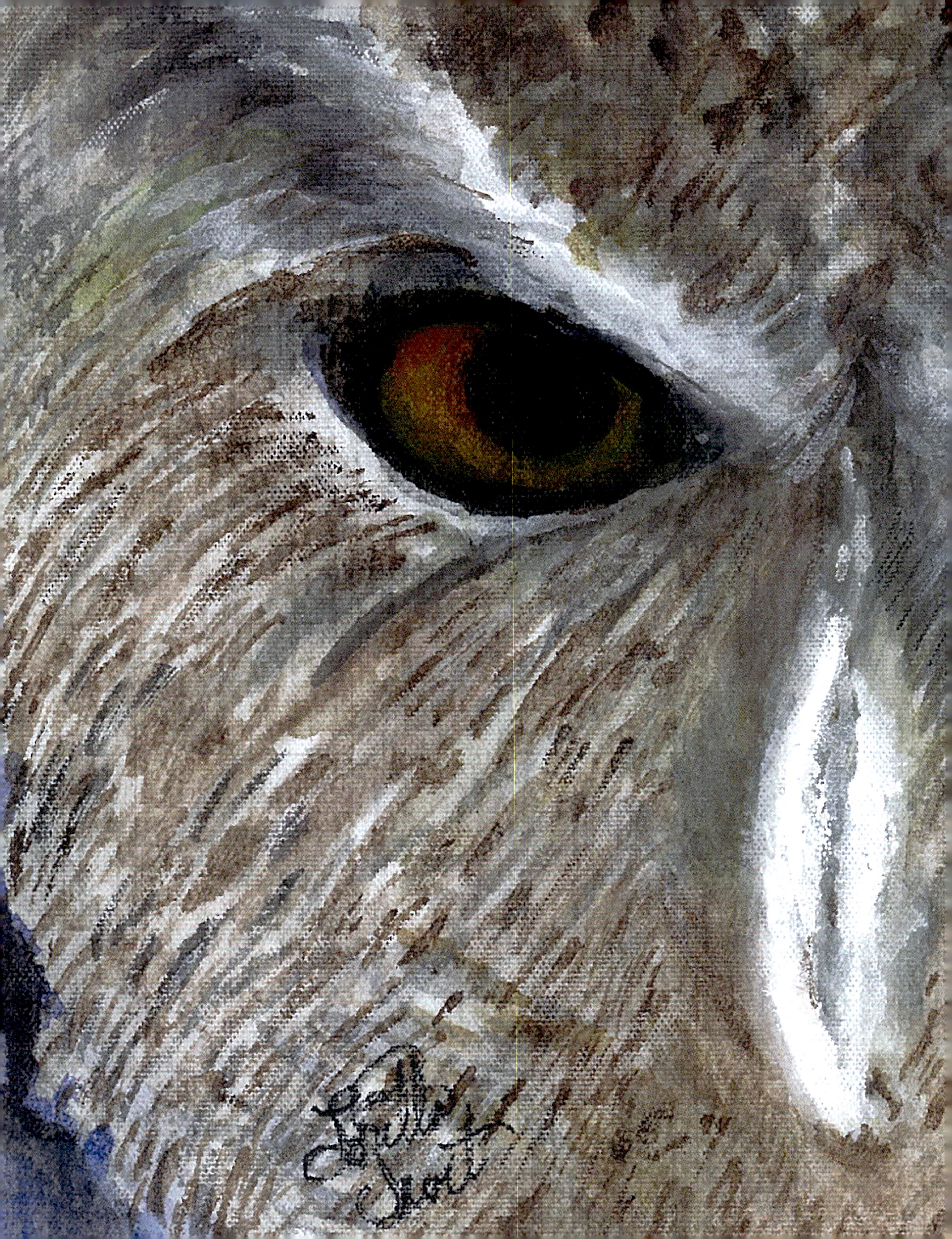

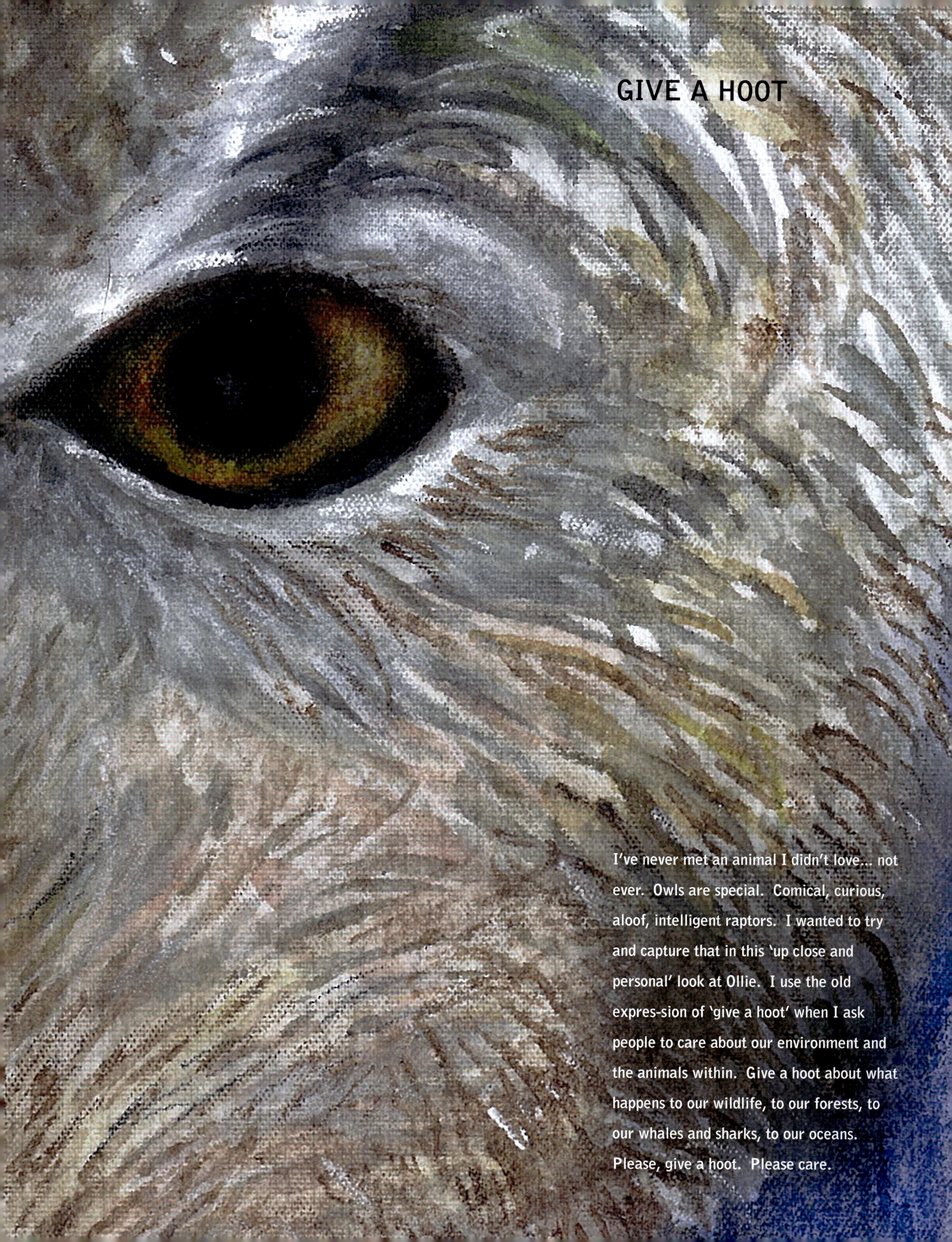

GIVE A HOOT

I've never met an animal I didn't love... not ever. Owls are special. Comical, curious, aloof, intelligent raptors. I wanted to try and capture that in this 'up close and personal' look at Ollie. I use the old expres-sion of 'give a hoot' when I ask people to care about our environment and the animals within. Give a hoot about what happens to our wildlife, to our forests, to our whales and sharks, to our oceans. Please, give a hoot. Please care.

SQUATTER'S RIGHTS

Here's my Yorkie with a baby kitten nestling comfort-ably on her head. "Charamusca" seems to be thinking it may not be such a great idea, but that if she tolerates it, may be there may be a little treat in store for her.

Her nickname is "Munchkin." Most of my friends call her "Munchie." Makes sense — a delicious little snack of a dog with a big loving personality. We refer to her as a "New-Yorkie"® because she is such a Big Apple/Central Park kind of dog. What a life! The kitten came from a thought in my head, an idea. She has no identity other than that of a sweet, adorable "Squatter."

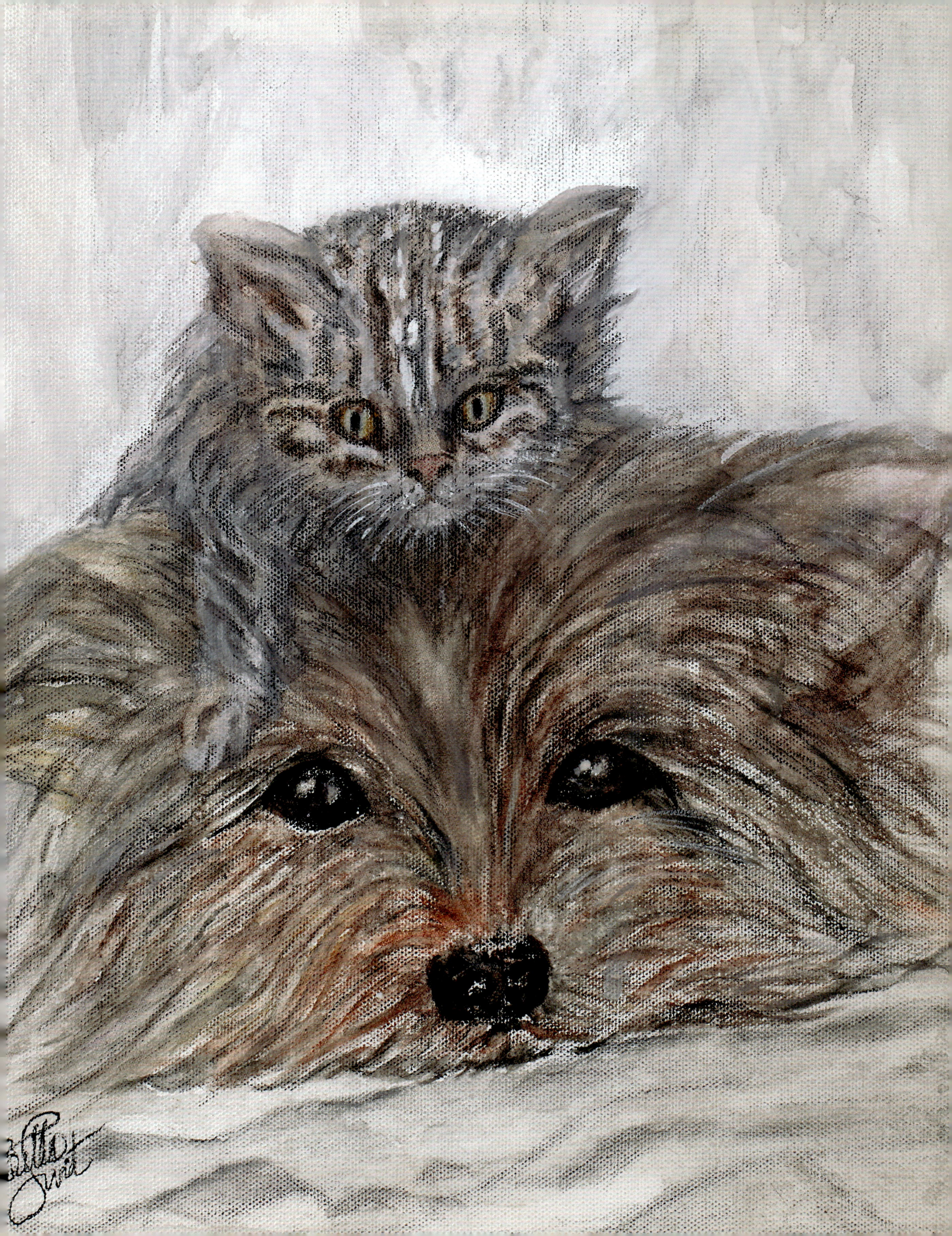

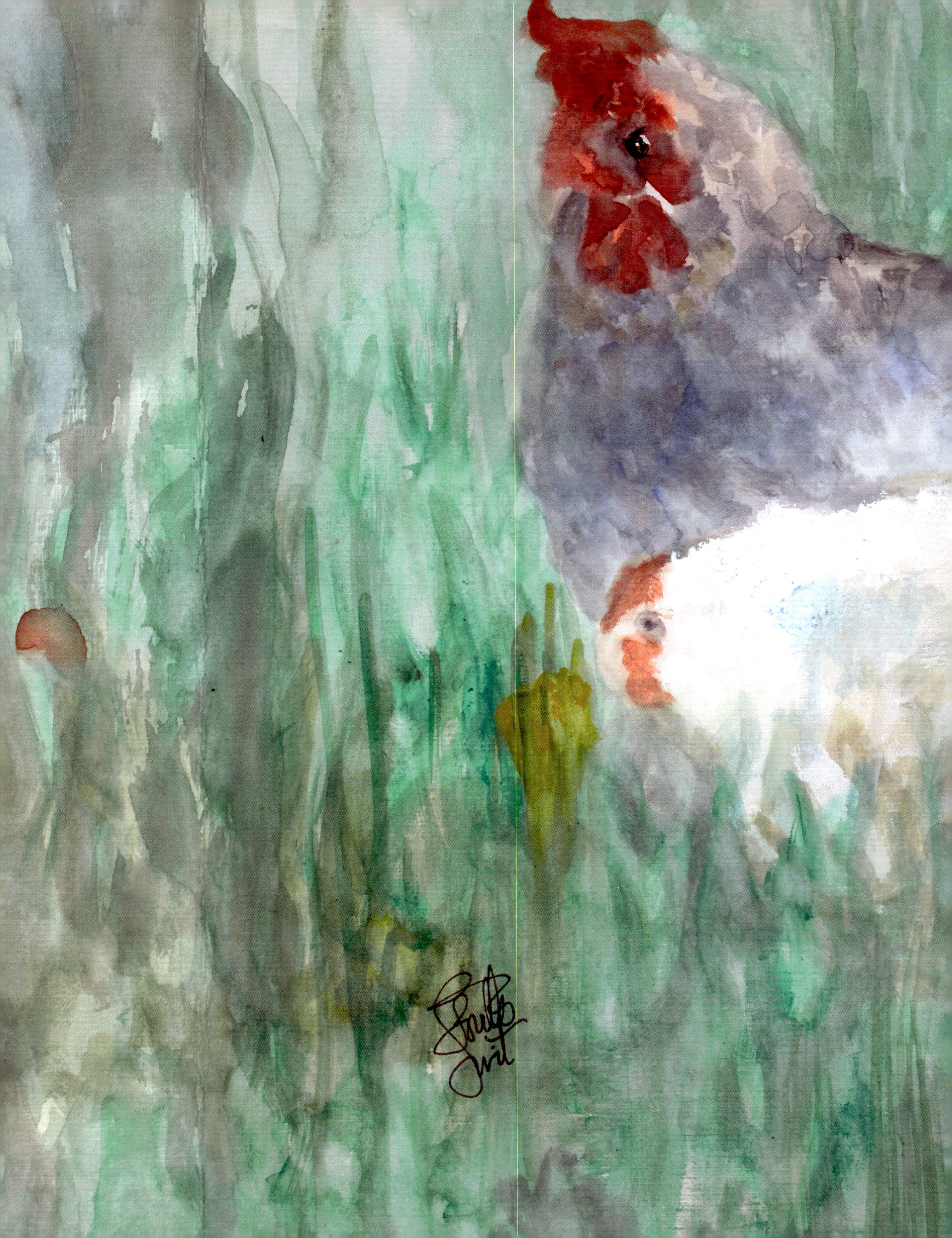

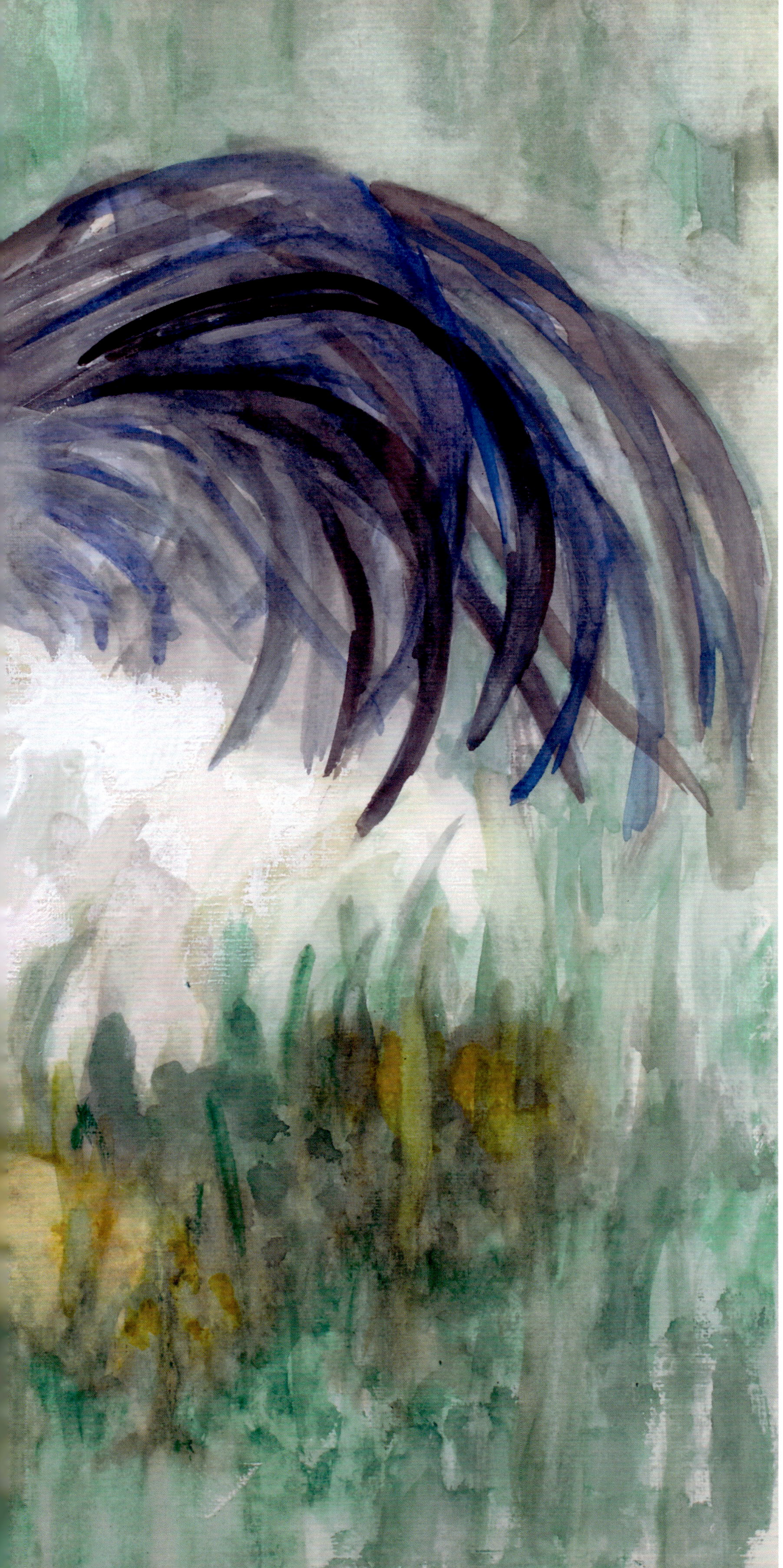

FAMILY STROLL

I'm so very proud of this painting.

It was ambitious, daring, presumptuous, and I did it anyway! The gentle idea of this family taking a leisurely stroll together......... it always makes me smile. The original hangs in my kitchen.

An artist friend liked it so much she asked me if she might use it as her computer screen-saver. She is a remarkable artist, and unlike my unschooled self, she has studied extensively for years and continues to do so.

It was a great compliment.

BOSSY NOVA

I thought my first chihuahua should be snappy and feisty and, well, sort of bossy. Into the mix there needed to be a grunt or two of Latin American style, so hence her name: 'Bossy Nova.' I see her always having her way with that pushy charm. Inspired by the more colorful backgrounds I had begun to paint, I went all out 'purple-fushia-hot' in accord with her snappy temperament; I topping off her flair with a deep blue collar. I most love the mauve reflection from the background on her skin.

She pops off the canvas in her bossy way.

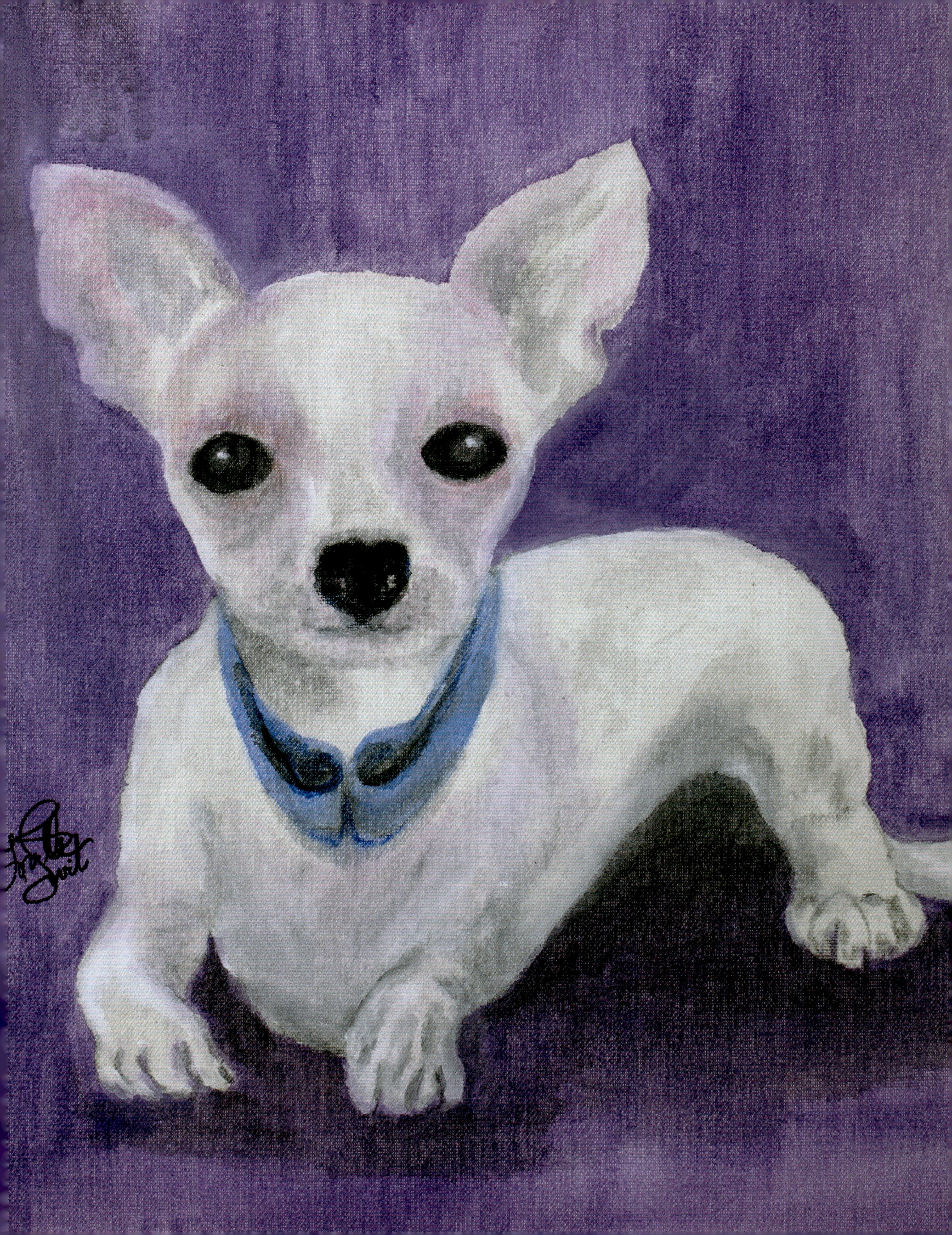

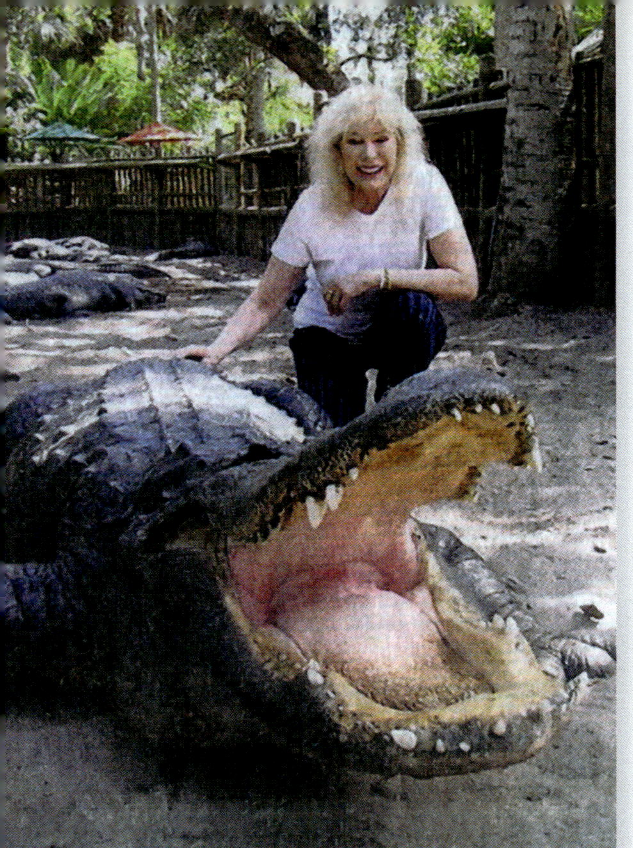

MY WILD LIFE WITH MY WILDLIFE

I was questioned as to the possessive, "MY" wildlife. Yes, I confess to the proprietary attitude I have towards all animals. It must be a mind-set. It never occurs to me they might hurt me. There I am being hugged by an orangutan and hugging a chimpanzee. The trainer, standing far behind the camera, was having anxiety attacks every time I cuddled the chimpanzee. Truth be known, primates are unpredictable, and they might've interpreted my hug as an attack. My friend Mike Henry, while playing Tarzan, had a working relationship with Cheetah, the chimpanzee in the Tarzan films. He was holding her in his arms when she suddenly bit deep into his chin. Streaming blood, he held his chin onto his face while trying to communicate to the non-English-speaking crew: 'Tarzan hurt... need doctor!' – Leave it to Mike to turn it into a funny story. Mike told me what had happened, but I could not keep myself from hugging them. Or climbing into an alligator pit, or letting that grizzly lick my face, or wrestle with a baby cheetah, or miss a photo-op with that enormous tiger. How can I not help feeling that they are, indeed, "Mine?"

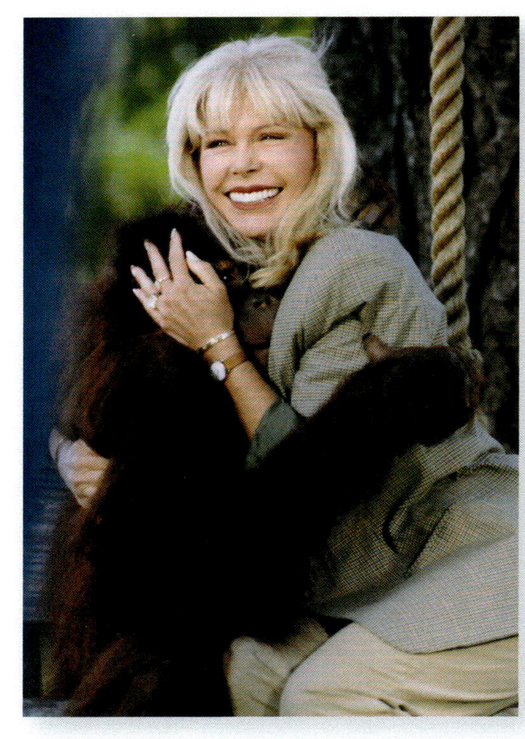

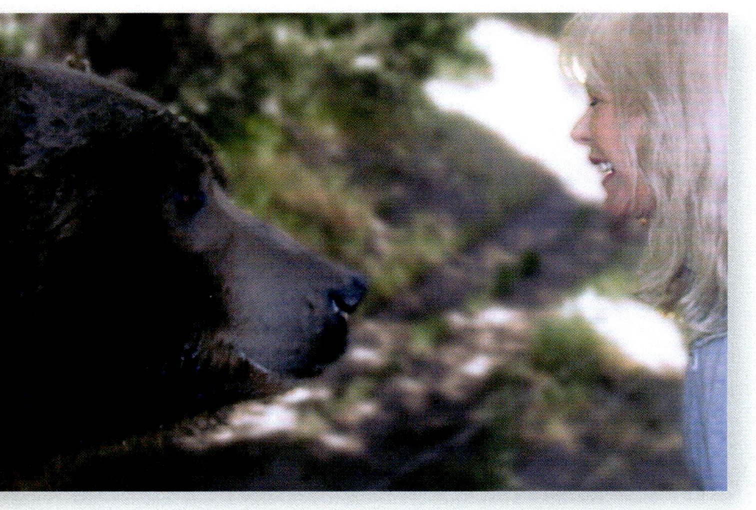

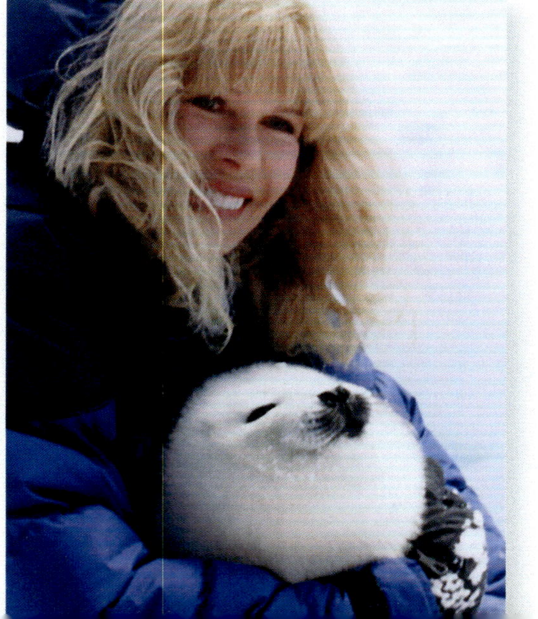

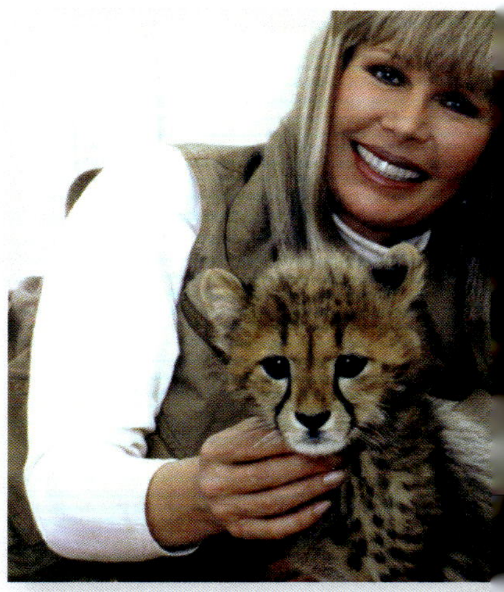

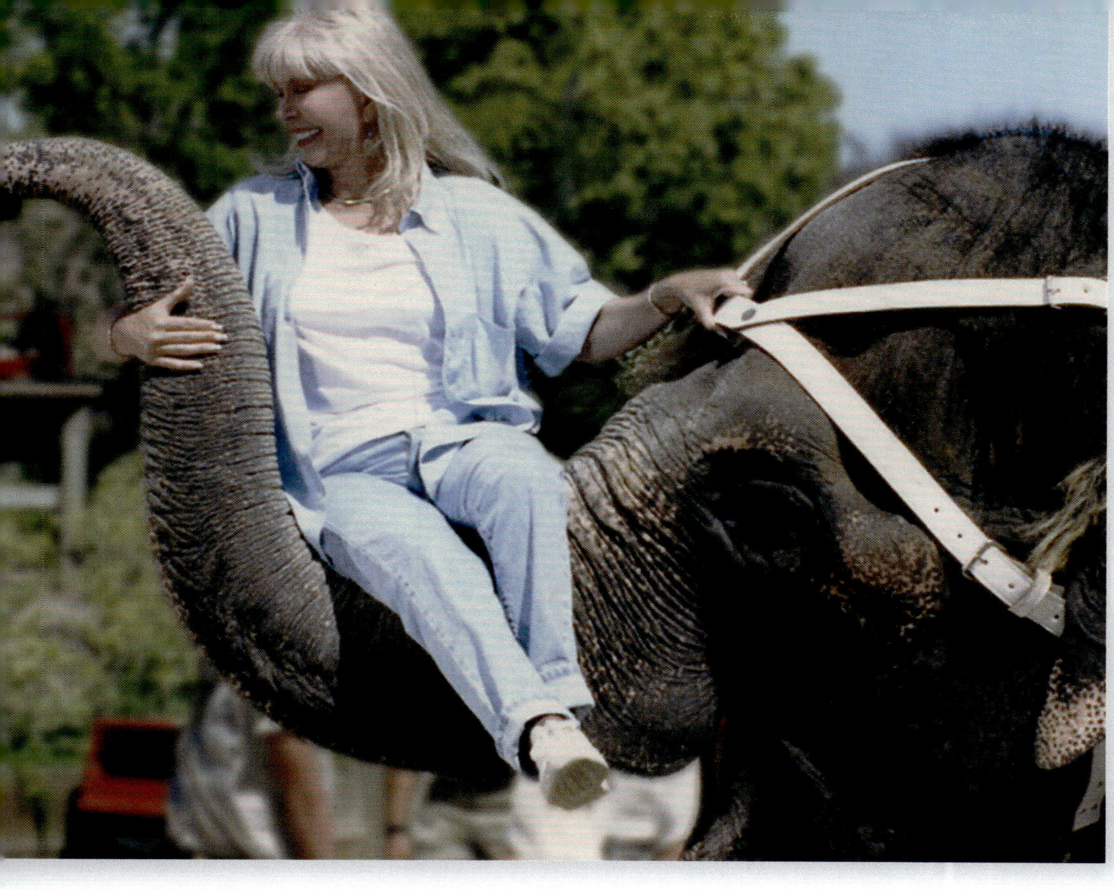
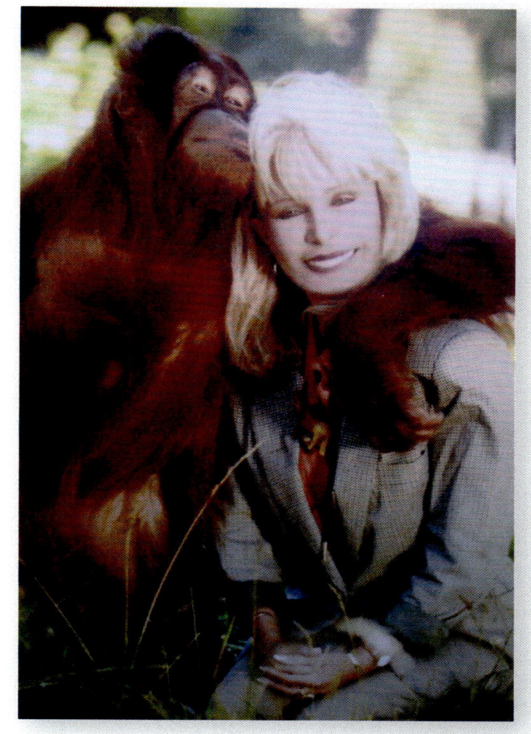
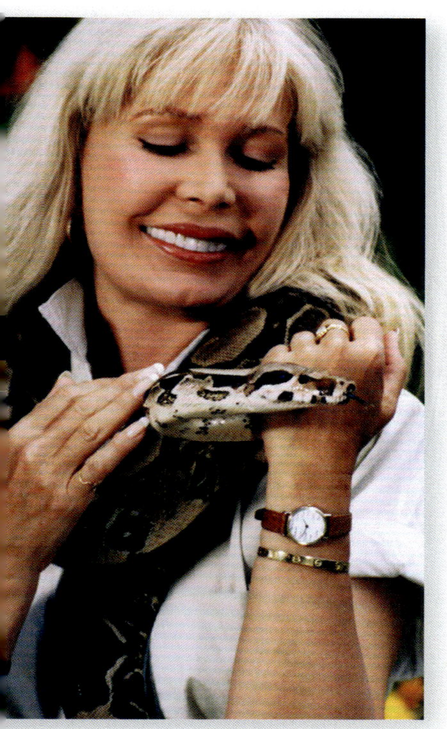
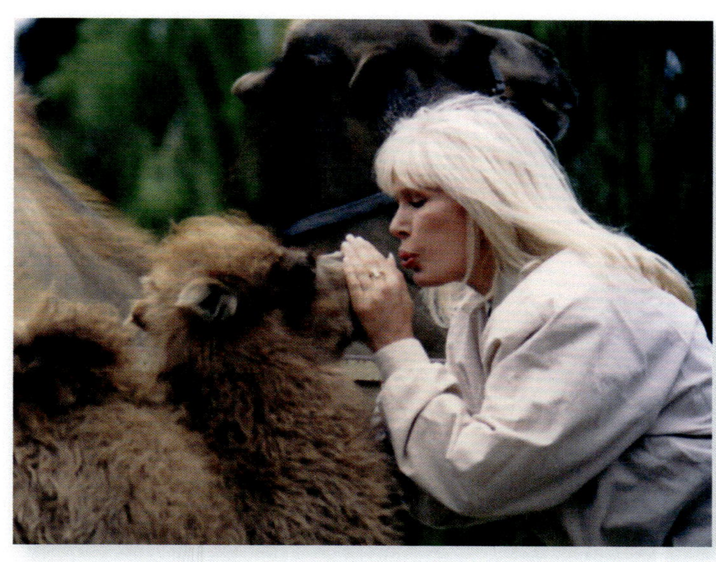
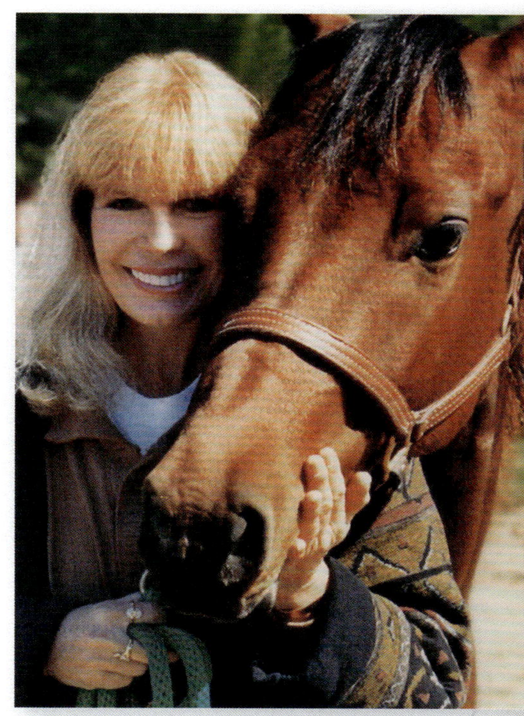
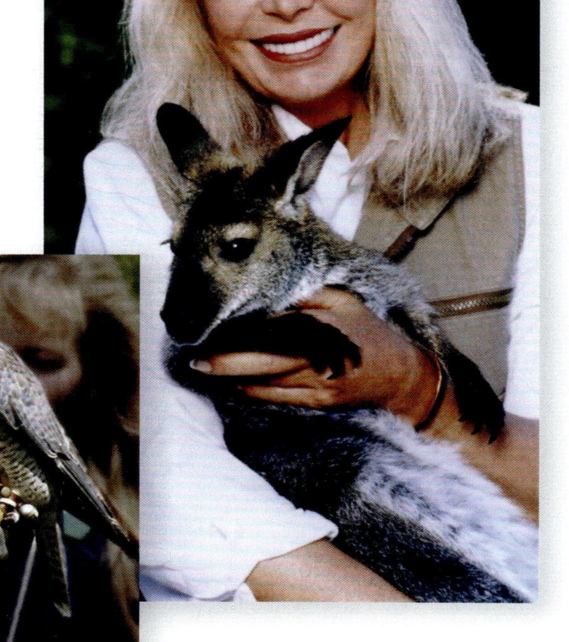
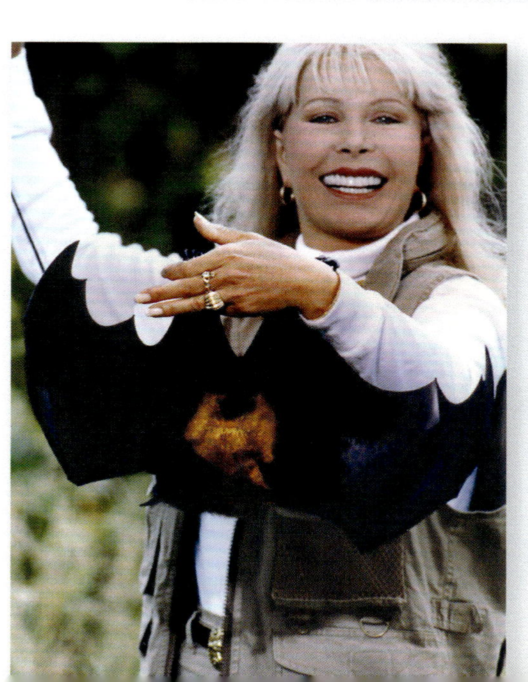

Most photos courtesy 'Those Incredible Animals', Discovery Channel

FELIX

I will always have a special place in my heart for Felix. He was one of the first felines I painted, and I did so as a gift for two great friends: amazing, generous activists, James Costa and John Archibald. We met at a fund-raiser for FARM SANCTUARY, an organization near and dear to our hearts. When I first saw Felix sporting those wonderful tiger stripes, I was more than a bit daunted. I kept telling myself that there are no problems — there are only challenges. Given that mantra, I have to say that Felix was quite the challenge. James and John were very happy with the painting. Seems little enough to give them for their untiring work on behalf of animals.

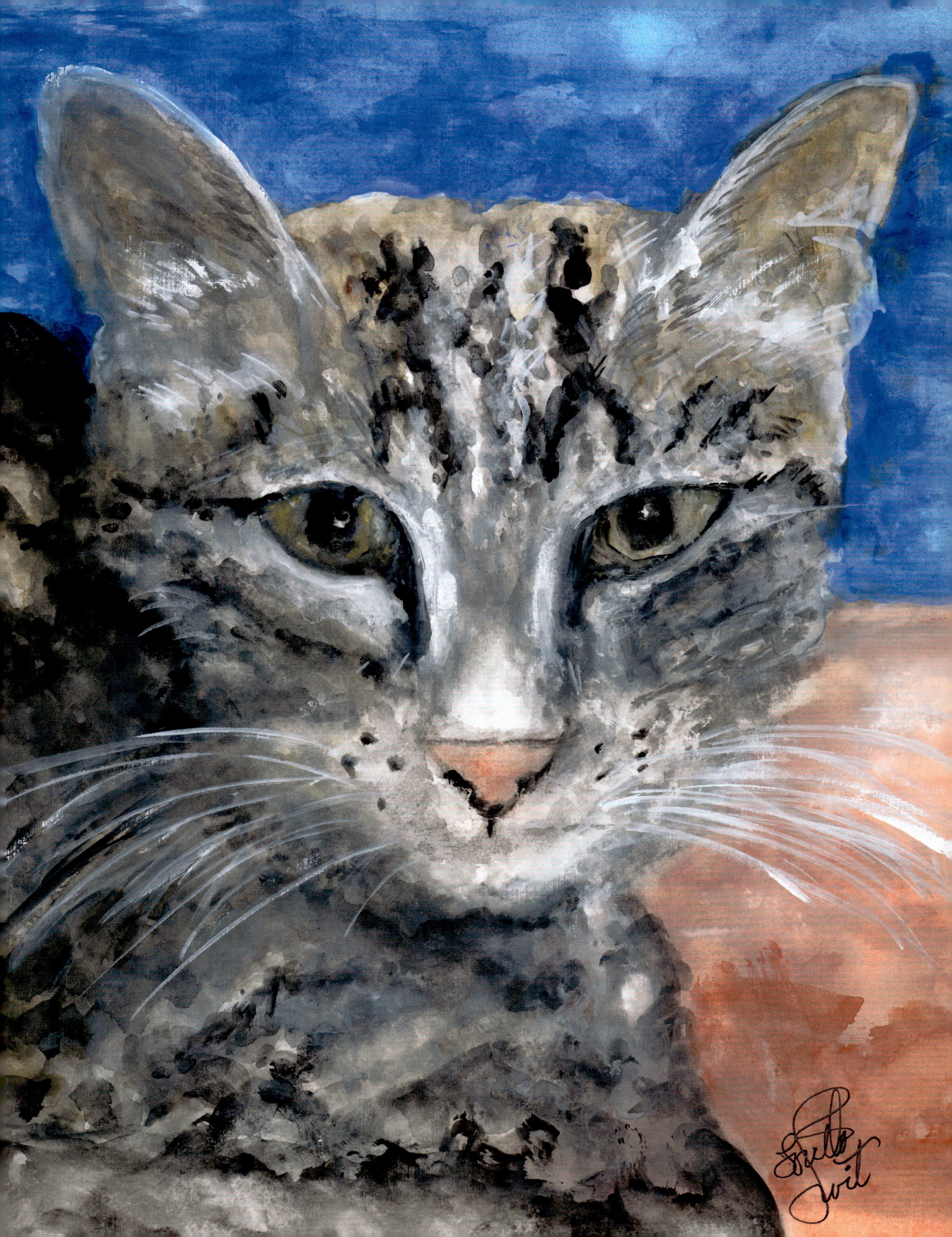

JELLY GLASS JAR

We made over 250 episodes of M*A*S*H and quite often I am asked in interviews to name a favorite or two. It's difficult to pick just one or two, I would say, but on deeper reflection, I realized that there was a favorite 'something' in each and every one of them: a scene, a joke, maybe a close-up. It occurs to me that I feel the same way about some of my artwork. I love the texture of the jar in this painting in much the same way that I love Cut Glass Vase (page 83.

Sometimes it's just the reflection in a cat's eyes, or the silky texture of his coat. Perhaps it's the very thing which inspires us to go on to the next work...... And the next.........

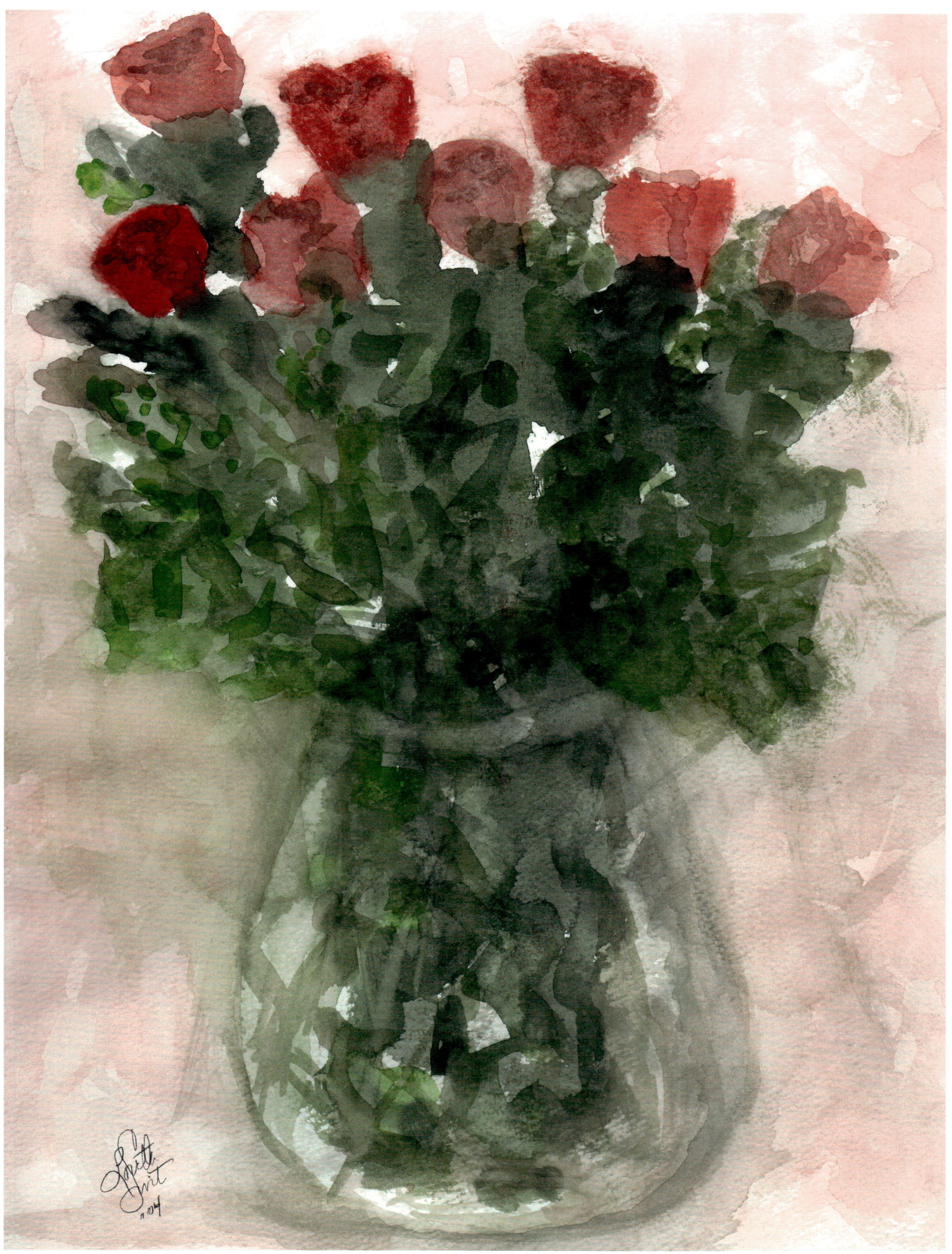

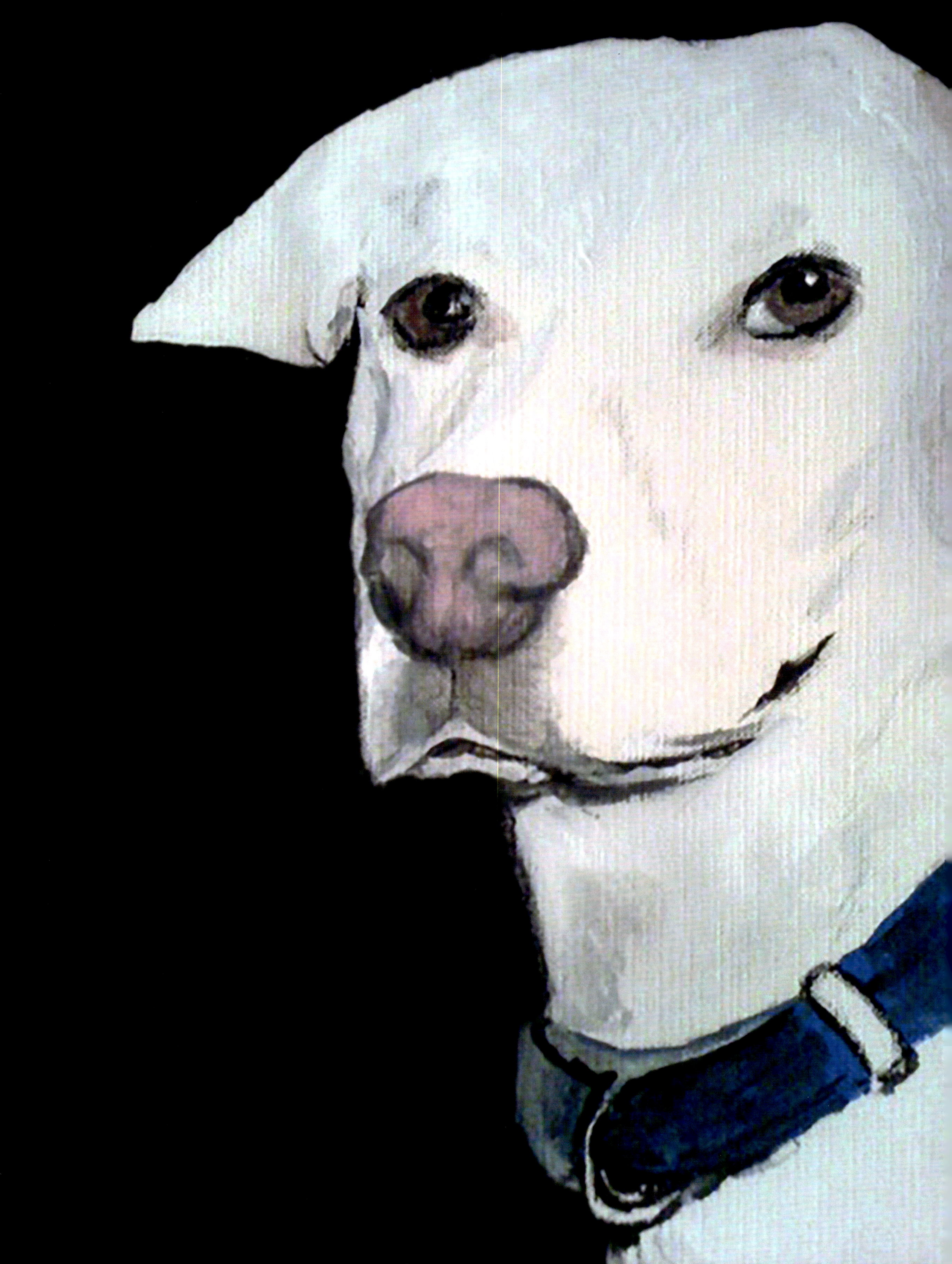

TIGGER

The beloved Hersch family member, Tigger, was entering his twilight years. Sherrin, a lifelong friend, approached me with the idea of gifting a painting of Tigger for her son's family. Would I paint it now, instead of waiting for the inevitable so that she'd be prepared to give the painting to her son's family at the passing of their beloved animal companion.

I worked from one of her favorite photos of Tigger. She jokingly calls him as "Tigger the Digger." He was an escape artist extraordinaire — tunneling was his specialty. Tigger was deeply loved and a very dear, close member of the family.

HENPECKED

Remember Henny-Penny who thought the sky was falling? Henpecked brought that dear children's story to mind.

Like the story, she's pure imagination and my own creation. Henny appealed to a dear friend of mine who happened to be visiting when I put the finishing touches on her.

Pun Intended: I call my friend's next move 'fowl play.' She took that painting for her own before the paint was dry! Henny still remains in her kitchen, beautifully framed, and she remains unapologetic about the theft!

That's fine with me because she has for years been a loving, supportive foul-weather friend.

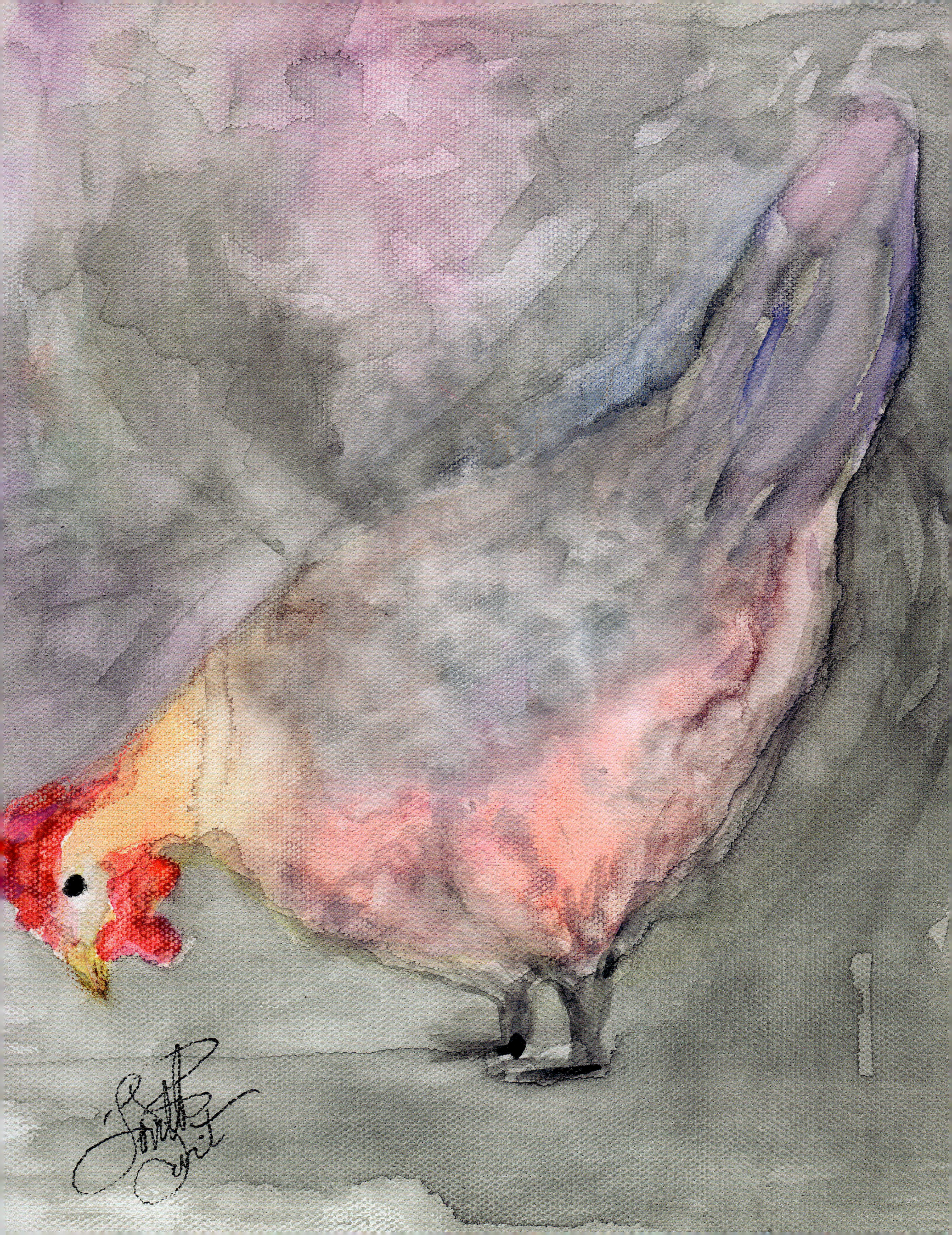

CLYDE

It was the first day of rehearsing 'Love, Loss and What I Wore,' that totally delightful piece about how, why and where we make associations with our wardrobe......... funny, poignant, honest and immensely entertaining.

One of my co-stars in the piece, Mary Testa, was flipping through her wallet. I happened to glance over and saw a photo of Clyde, a sweet little Min-Pin. 'Mary,' I said, 'he's a painting!'

I asked her to give me a few photos in different poses, and I went to work.

I met him soon afterwards, a sweet little energetic miniature Pincher.

Here he is in all his "feisty-ness."

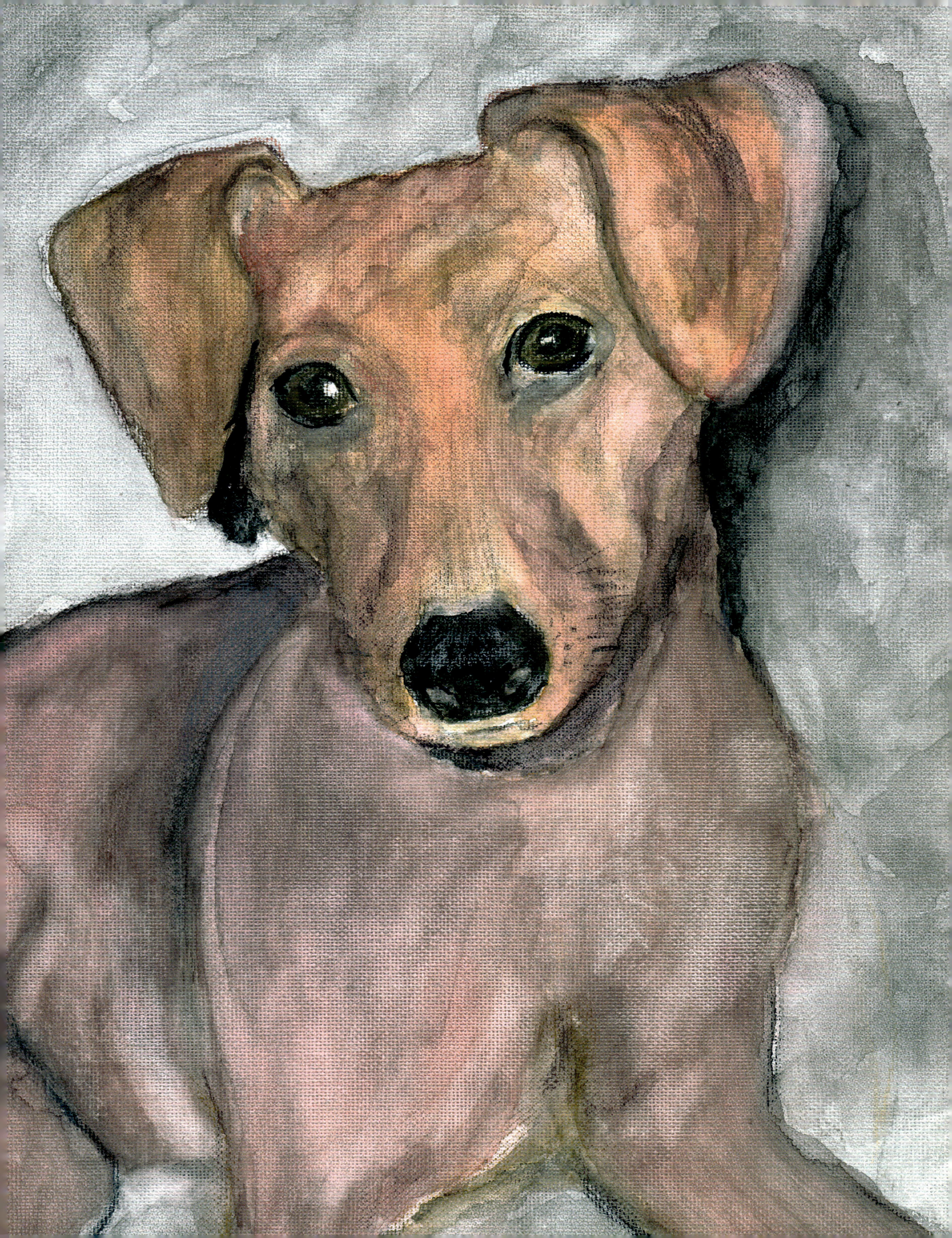

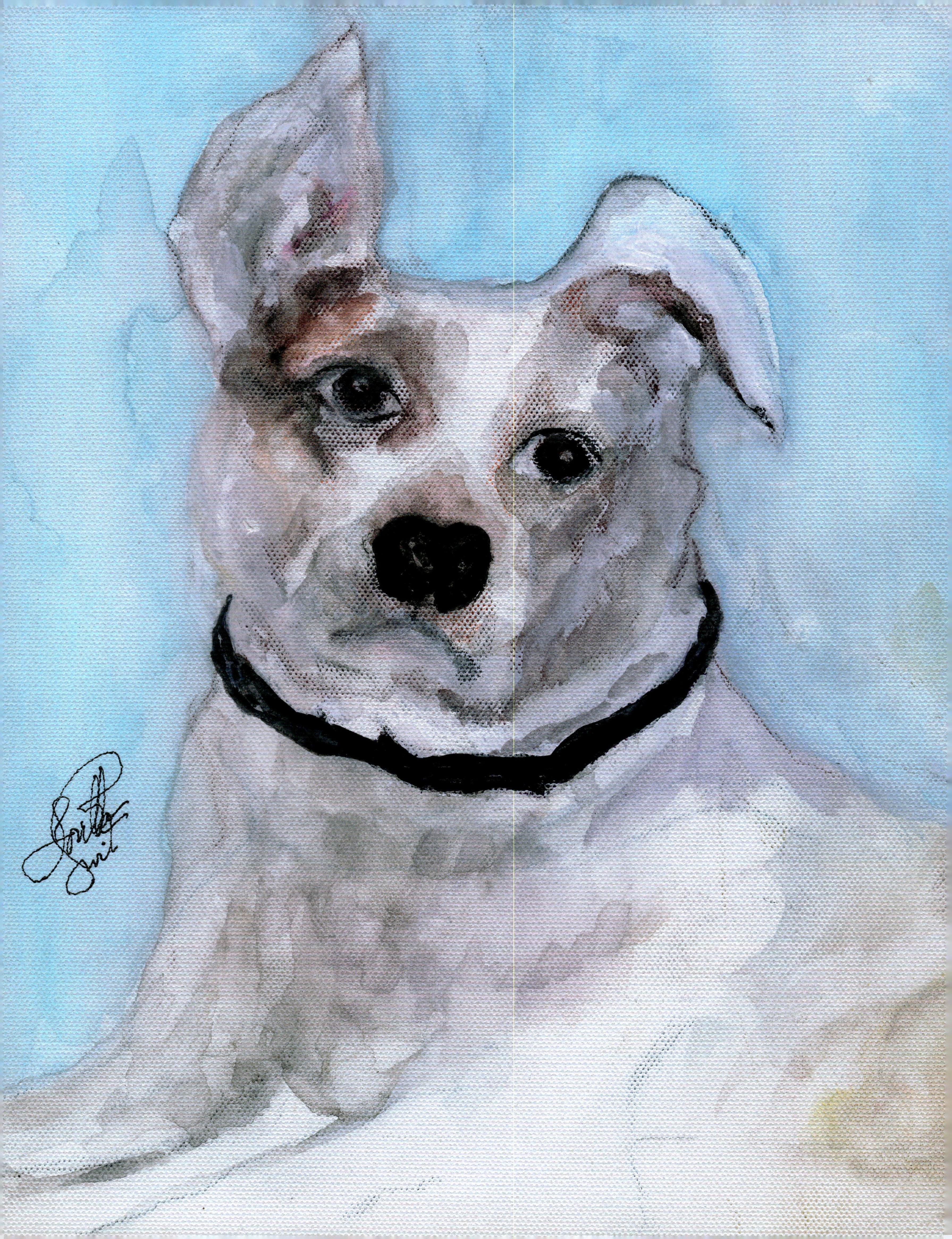

REALLY?

Perhaps "the master's voice" was more appropriate. I just felt so certain that he was being 'upped' from a nap to play 'Fetch' with the visiting family children. He'd be amenable in a second.

That's how dogs are......... so eager to please. I'd like to think I caught him at that moment of being a bit unprepared to rouse himself for what, (I am convinced) he thinks is a pointless game.

Treats are much more fun.

L'AUBE

Somewhere in the windmills of my mind, I must have registered the look of a flower like the one bending gracefully from the jar. It may have been at the Sunday Flea Market, a place I love for finding unexpected treasures. It's one of my favorite haunts......... a great spot to forage and find.

To this date, I feel L'Aube to be some of my best work — one that I'm not likely to ever part with. It set a standard for me.

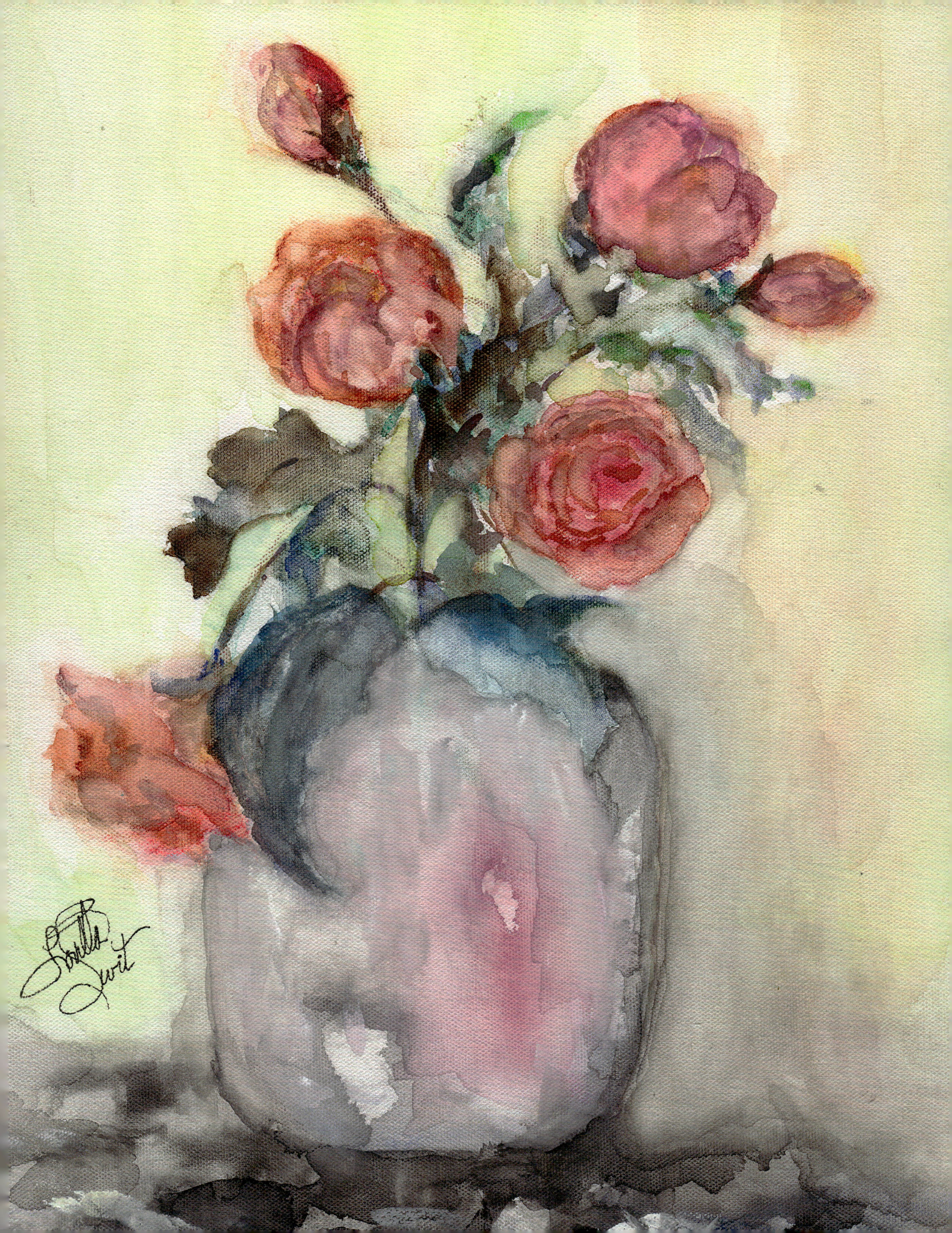

SUDAN

The leopard camouflage is so incredible that I found myself staring at the spot in the bush where my Masai guide was pointing for what must've been fifteen minutes. My eyes felt glued and frozen to the spot. Then suddenly, I realized I was looking into his green eyes. Slowly the rest of him took shape. He took my breath away......... literally. If he'd been closer, he might truly have actually taken my breath away.

The big cats kill prey to eat, feed their cubs and survive. Not so the leopard, I'm told. He kills indiscriminately.

I respect his DNA. After all, it's his home.

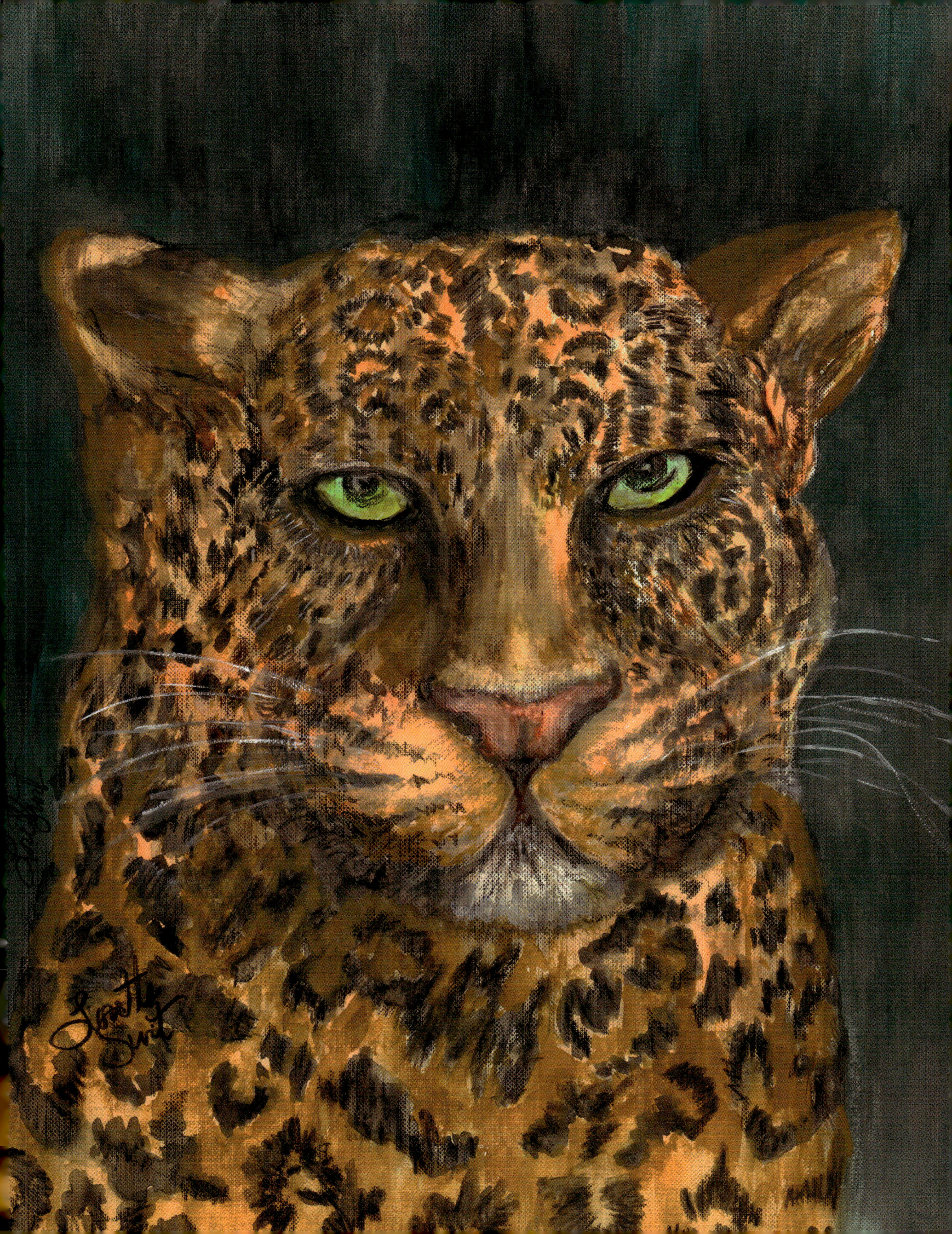

ROXIE

This painting was a major breakthrough in trust for me — trusting the sienna-rust color around her eyes, trusting the point of a brush to do that delicate mouth in one stroke, the hairs on her coat, and those amber-colored eyes.

I love this painting. I learned to trust the colors I see. It taught me to be bold.

Roxie made me very brave.

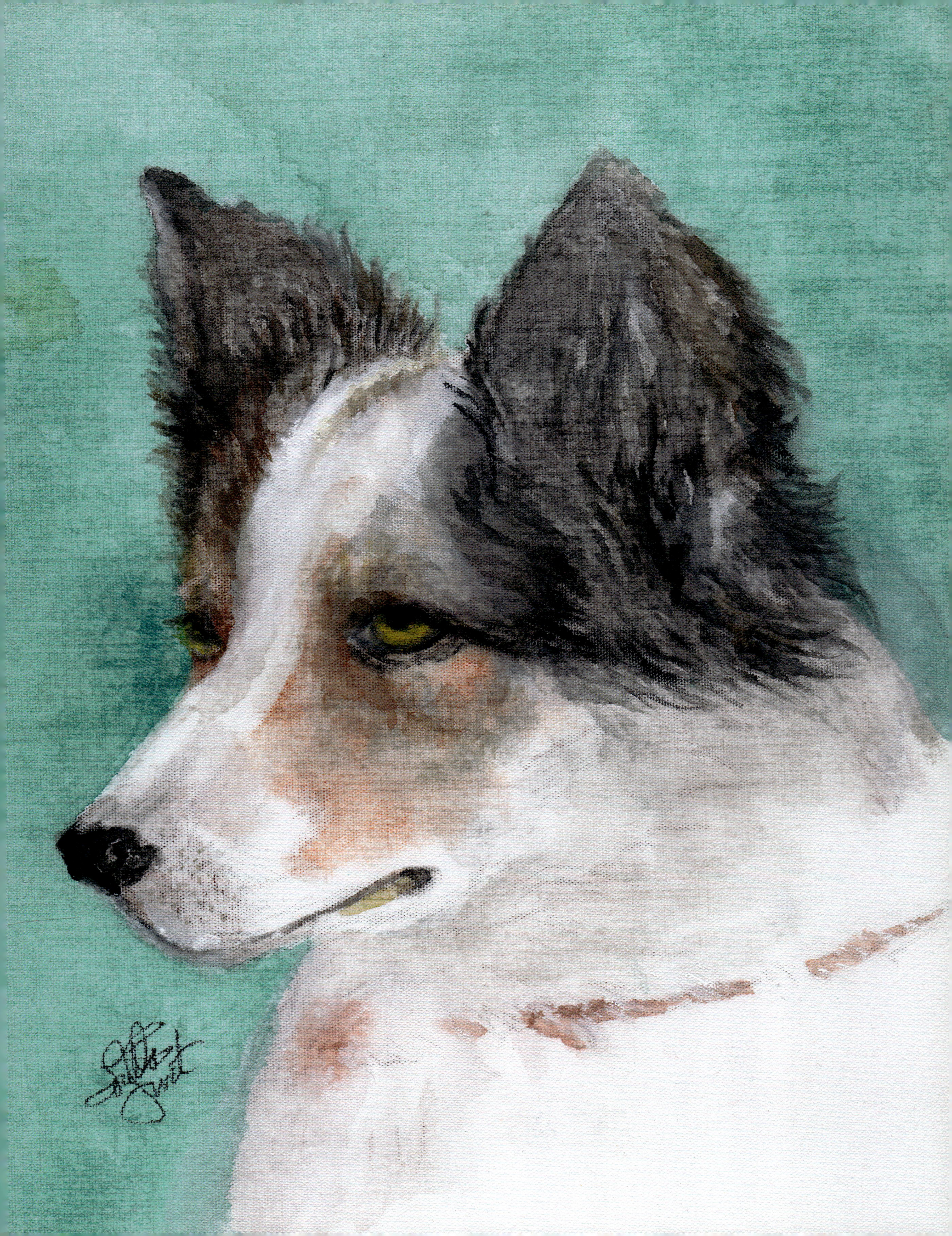

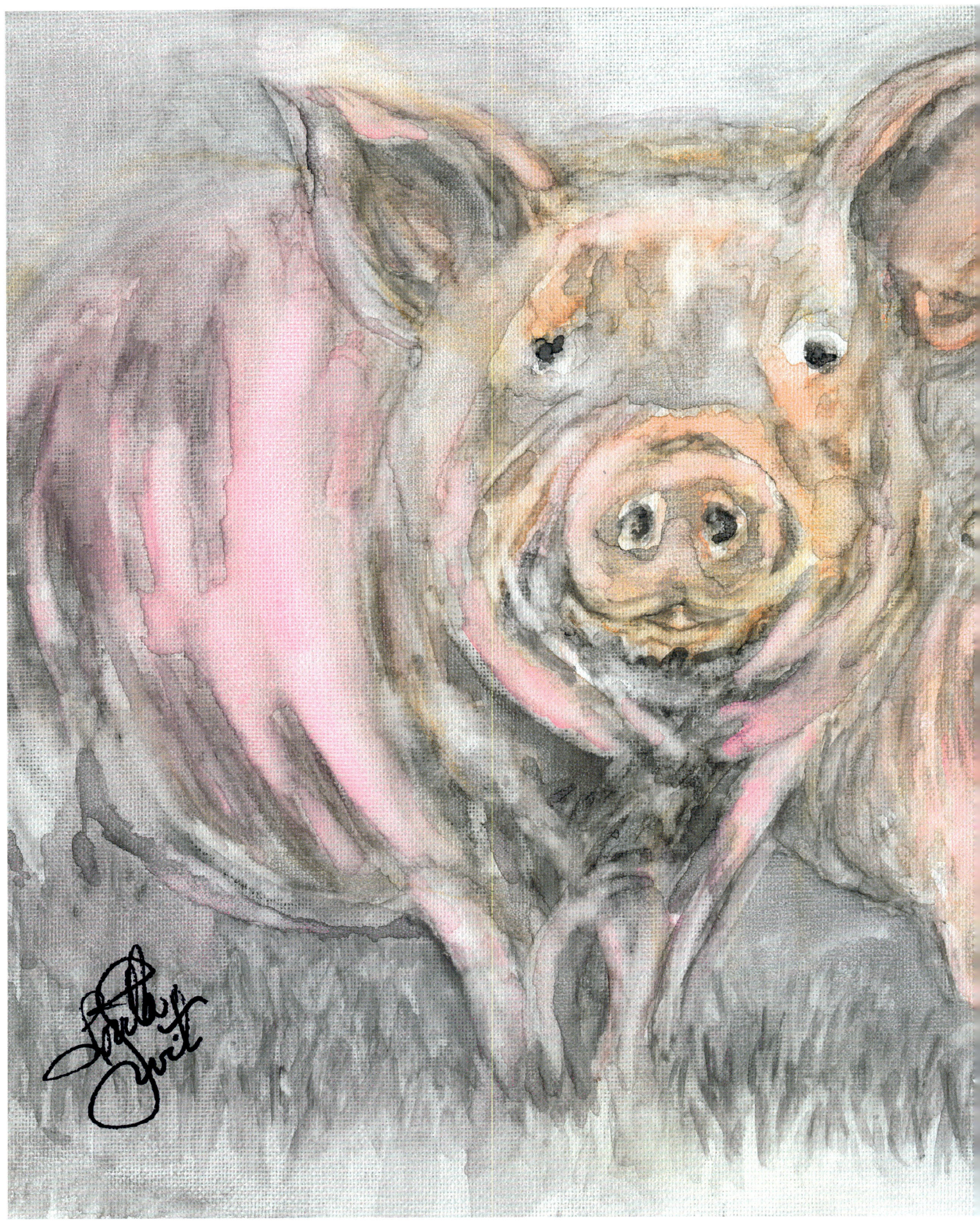

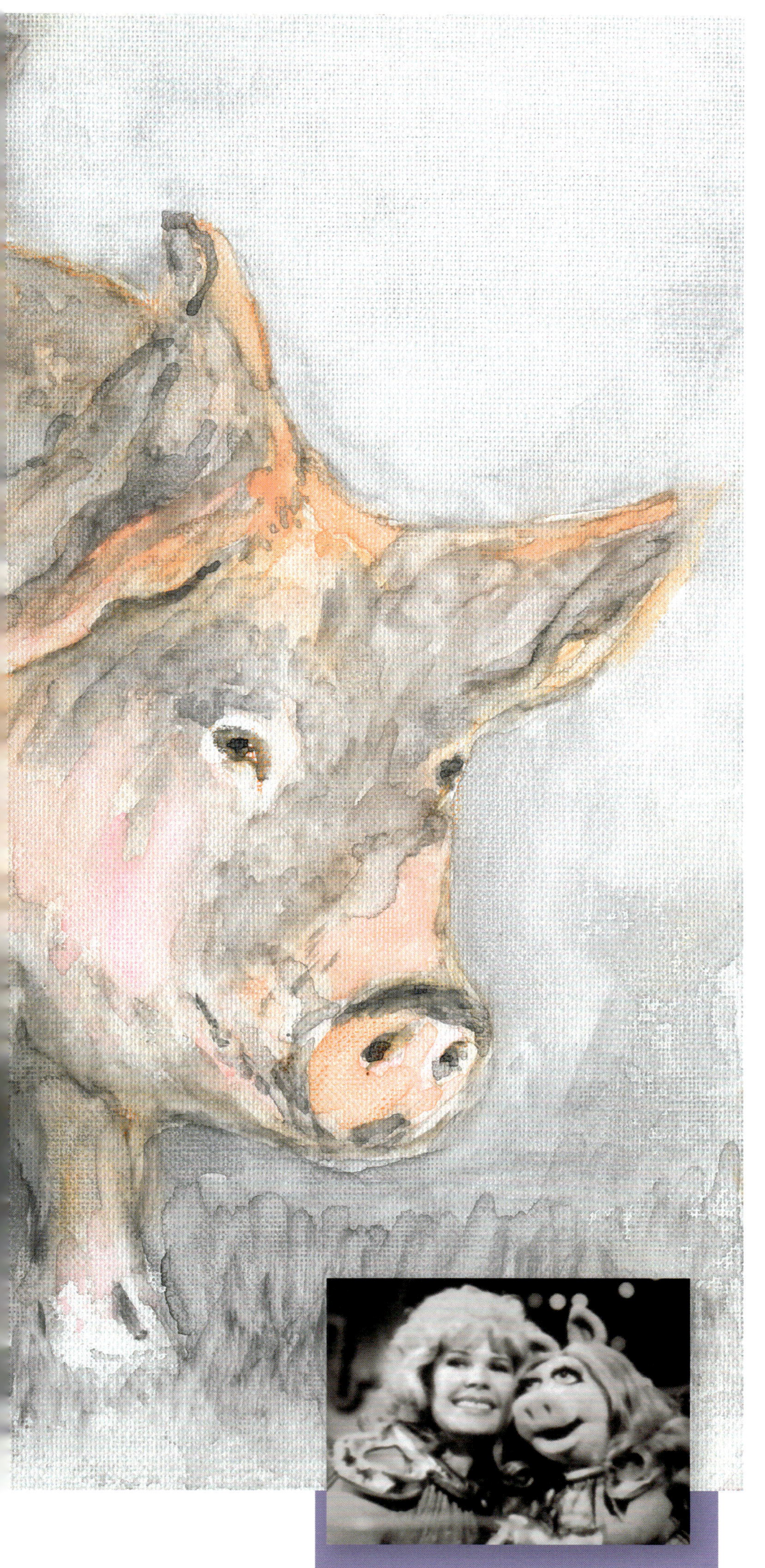

TWO OUT OF THREE

The muzzles of pigs and cows are very challenging. Since challenges help us stretch, I chose to paint two piggies out of the familiar nursery-rhyme-three. These particular ones live at the FARM SANCTUARY in peace and harmony with all the other farm animals. If you want a great party, call the Sanctuary and put your name on the Evite list. You might want to come up at Thanksgiving-Time to feed the turkeys and enjoy the Vegan food — a wonderful time for a really great cause.

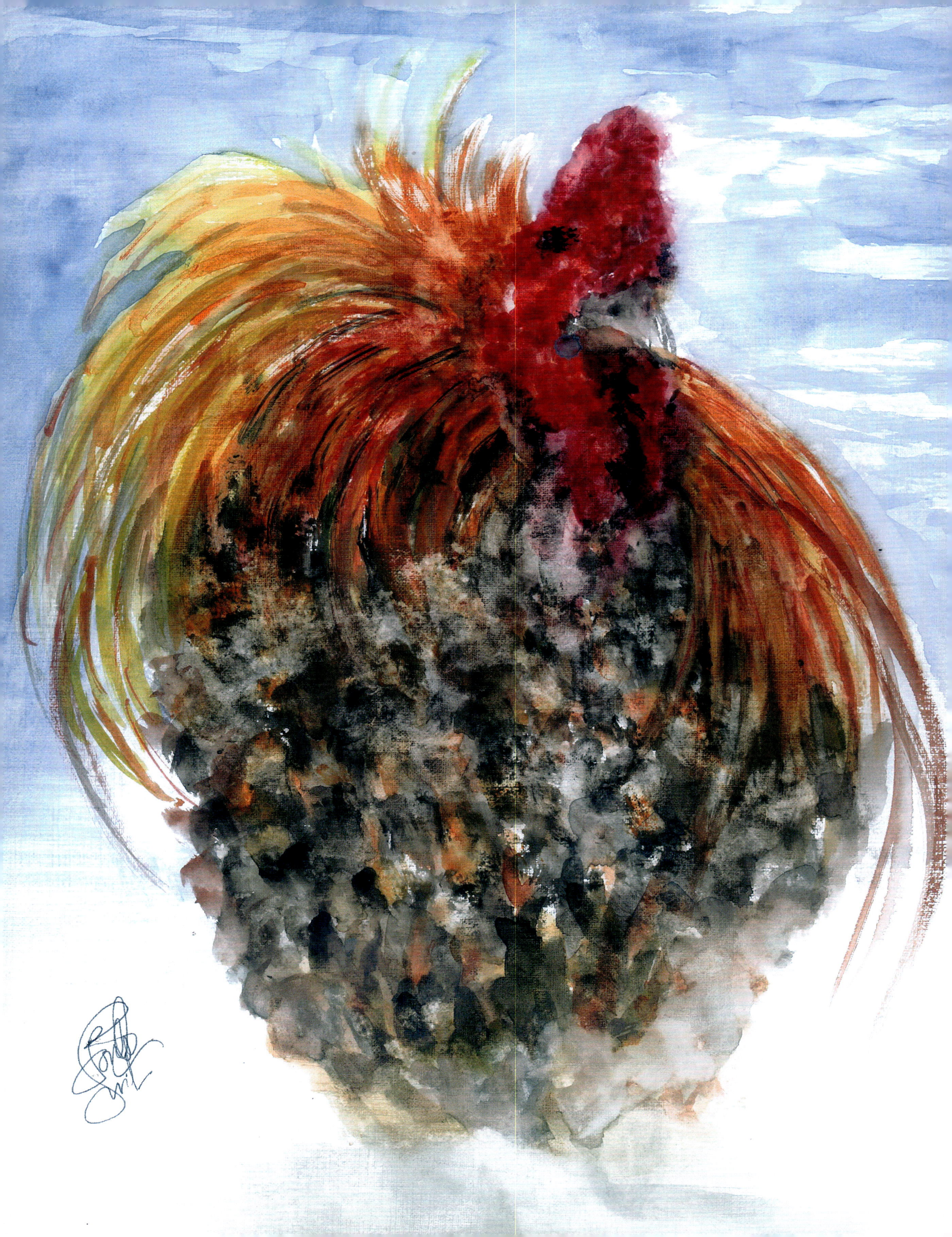

GLORIOUS

I was in Romania when I painted this magnificent turkey. I still marvel at the feathers and the colors. As difficult as it was, I felt driven to complete this painting. As always, when I travel, I bring my paints and canvas with me, along with a folder of ideas, photos, doodles and sketches for potential inspiration. When I chose Glorious, it was more like a moment of madness! It was certainly the most ambitious project I had ever faced. It took a lot of time, but I had the time.

Of all my work so far, I think Glorious most clearly demonstrates how brave I can be when I don't know what I'm doing. I didn't know enough to be intimidated and overwhelmed! Moving on in defense of my ignorance, I can now admit to an amount of learning I acquired with each painting, if only by osmosis.

CUT GLASS VASE

This is an early, oh, so early, piece of "Swit-Art." I wish I had dated my work as I progressed. I would guess that this painting was done in the 1980's, or thereabouts. I considered it then to be a breakthrough moment in achieving a sparkling cut-glass vase.

I remember being so proud and excited with the effect. I'm guessing further that I rushed to finish it so that I could show the vase to my friends and critics. As a result, I neglected the flowers.

I'm including this painting in the book to give myself 'E' for Effort and 'P' for Progress."

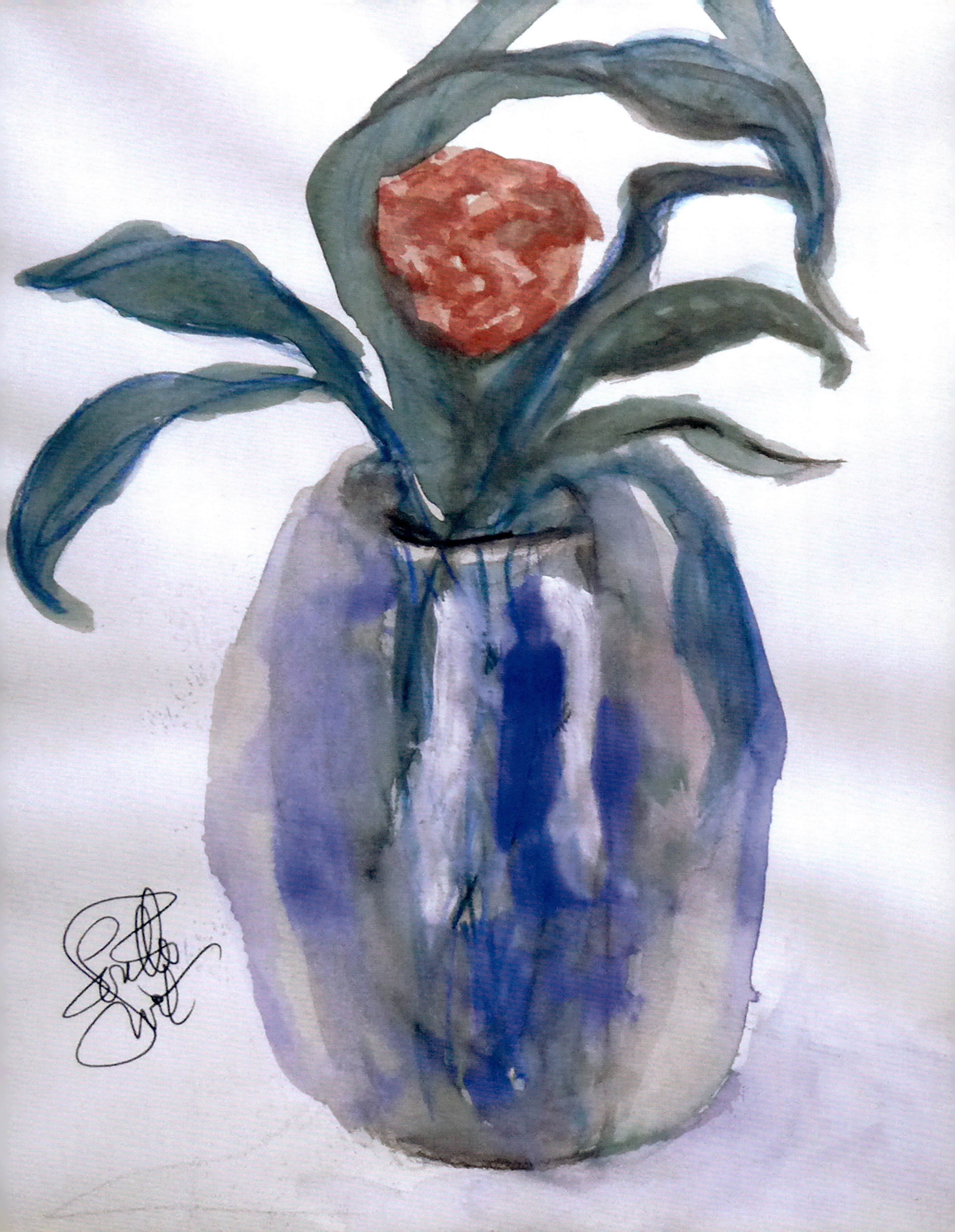

BIDE-A-WEE RUSSELL [book cover painting]

This endearing Jack Russell was a BIDE-A-WEE rescue. Allow me a moment to praise the work of New York City's oldest animal/rescue humane organization. I love those folks! Just recently they helped me rescue this adorable litter of sweet babes, taking them in at their Hampton Shelter, where they vetted and gave them shots, socialized them, and prepared them to be adopted out to caring, loving, forever homes, which had been thoroughly checked, accident-proofed and well-documented.

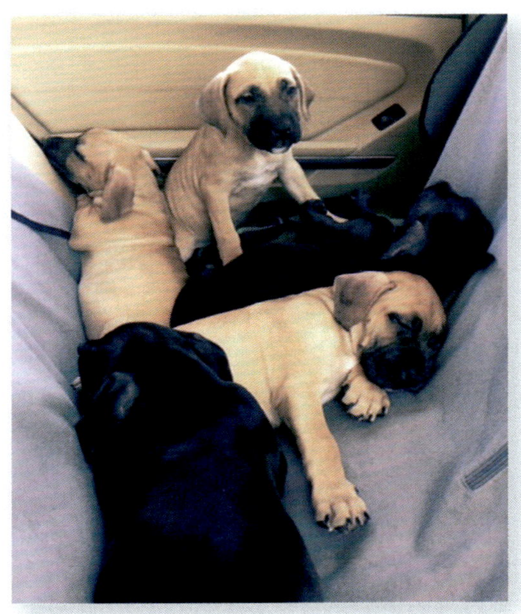

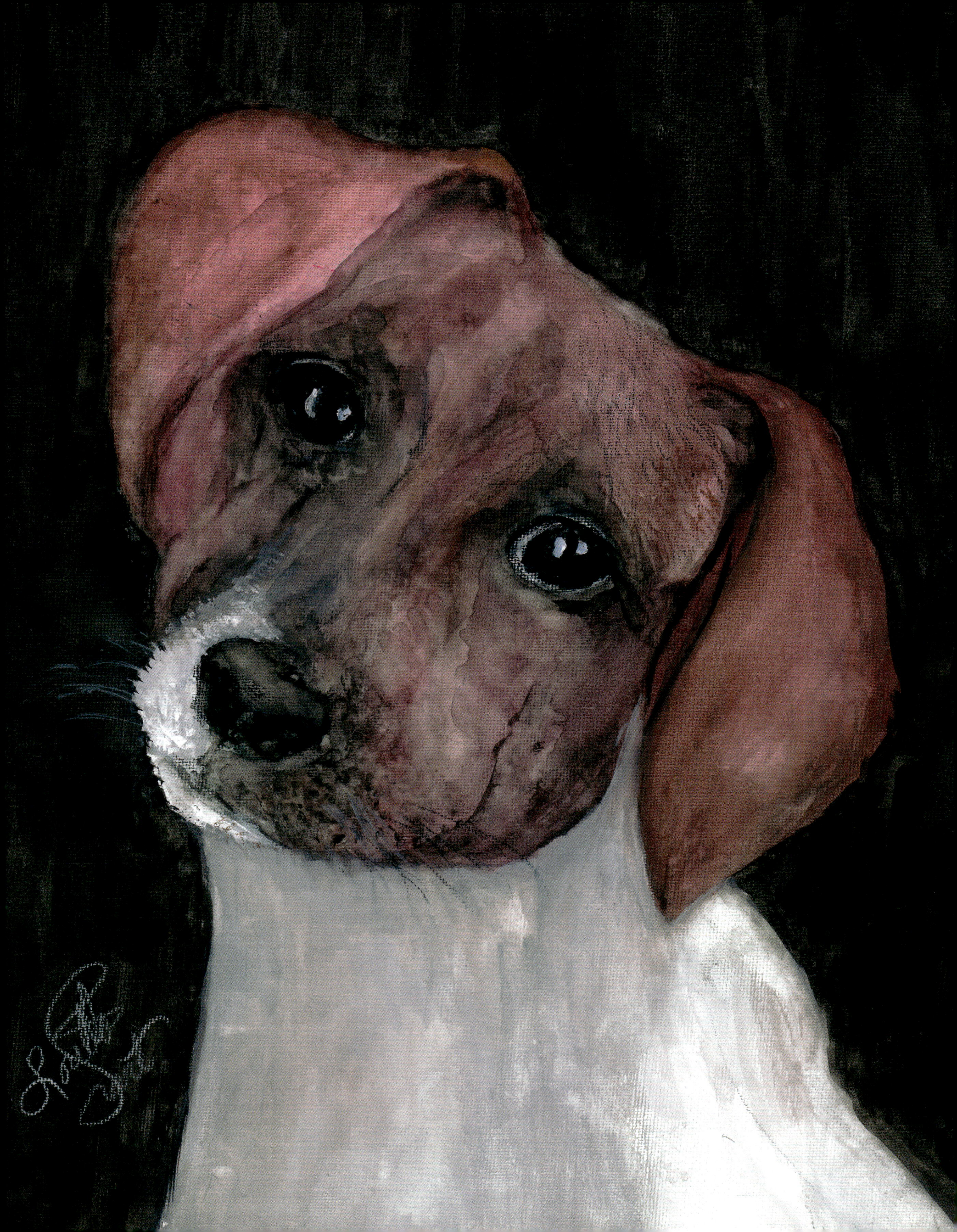

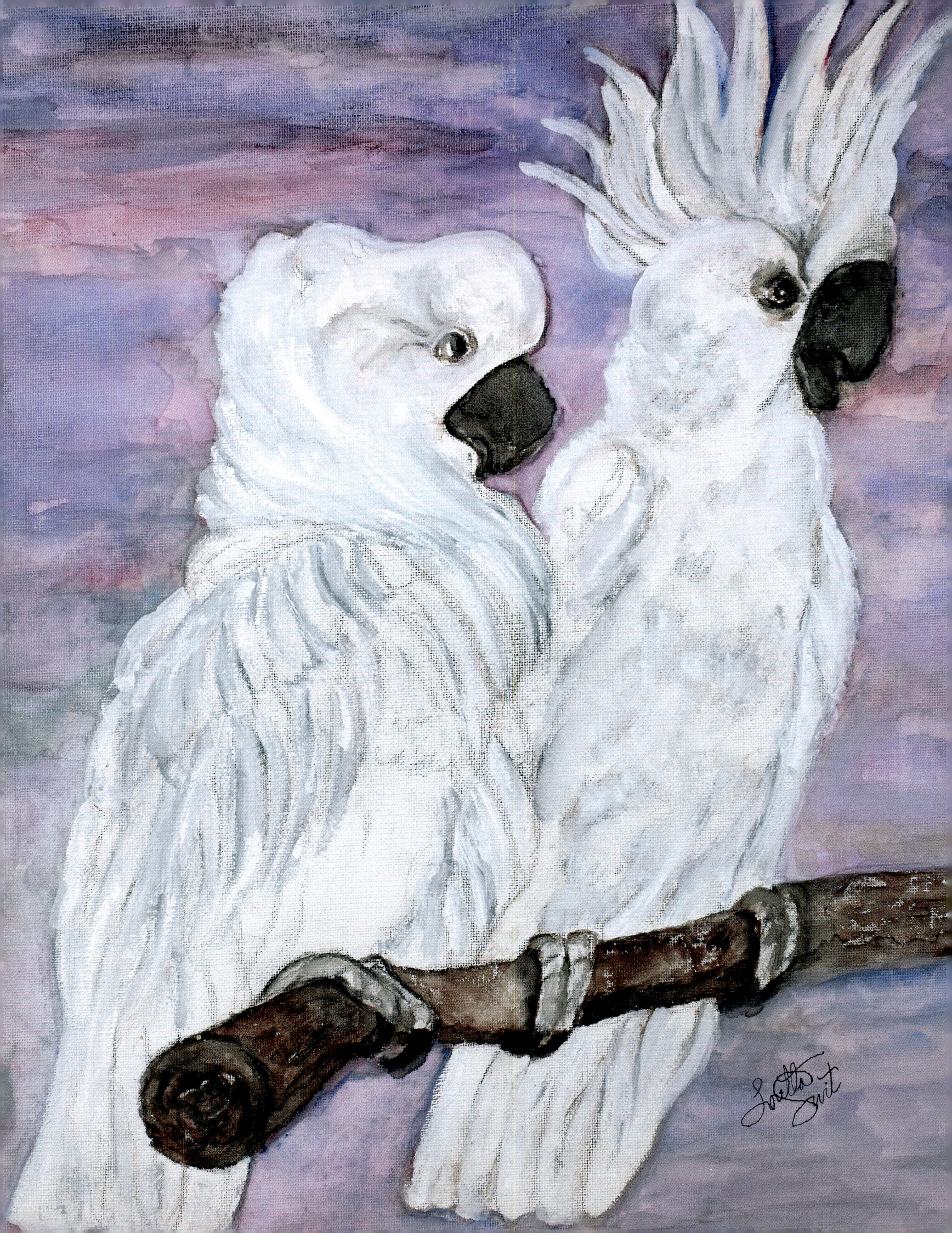

COCK-A-TOO TIMES TWO

I saw a B&W drawing of these two birds and decided to put some color into their lives. I tried for a glorious sunset. I once flew from Jamaica into Miami on a flight the airline had christened The Sunset Flight. It was dazzling. You felt as if you were flying directly into pools of magenta, gold and cerise......... flying through streams of color so vibrant that surely the plane would be streaked with those colors when it landed. A veritable artist's canvas — The Sunset Flight from Montego Bay to Miami.

VANILLA

I was so taken by the creamy, soft tones of this lovely little guy that I couldn't resist the challenge. He looked like an ice cream sundae, whipped cream and all. I thought his disposition matched his coloring as well, hence the name.

It's always a challenge to work in such light tones. I learned early in the game that 'white' as we know it, is not a color of nature, and I learned about using negative space.

Art, like life, is a learning process. That's why it can be so exciting.

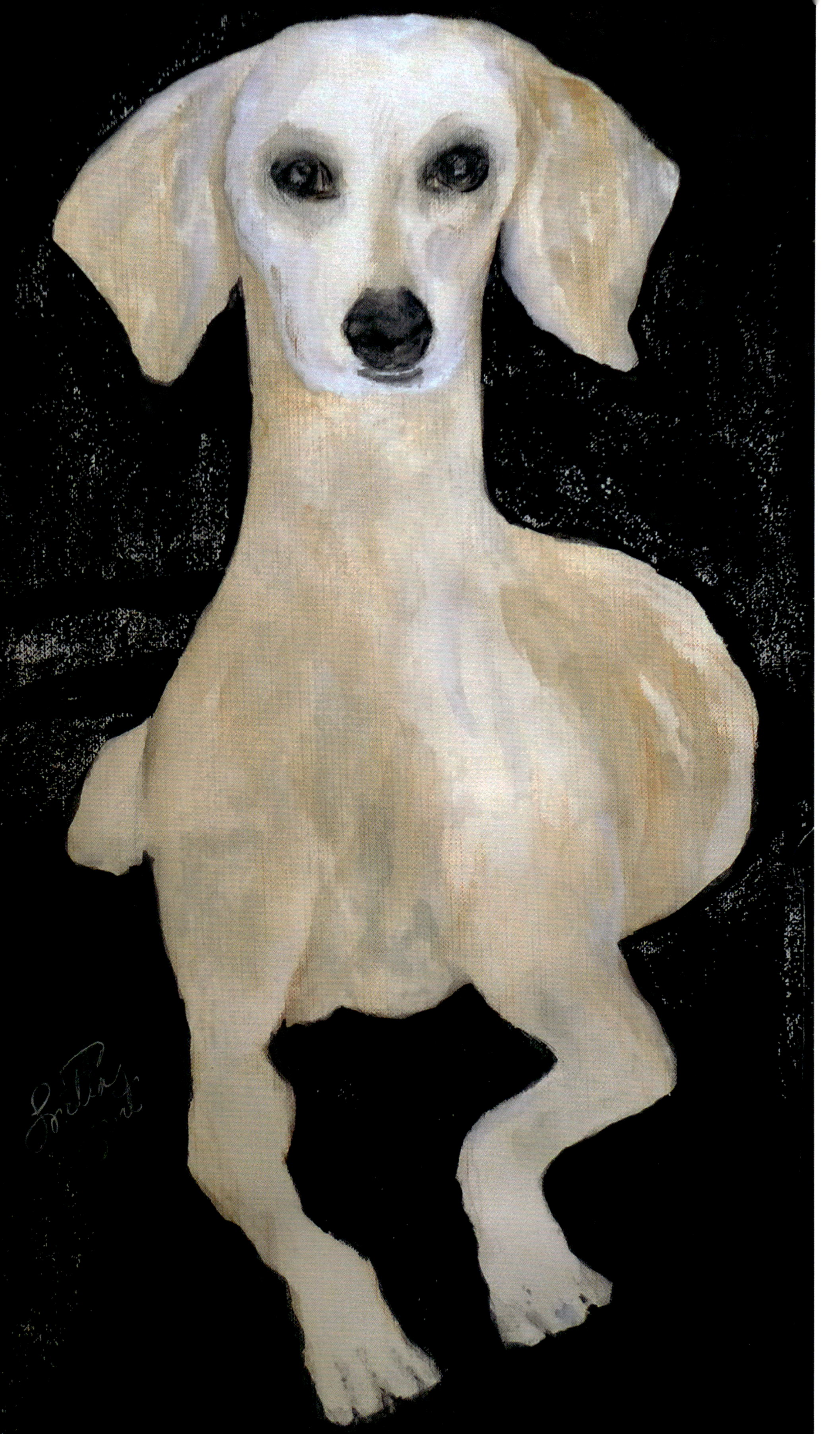

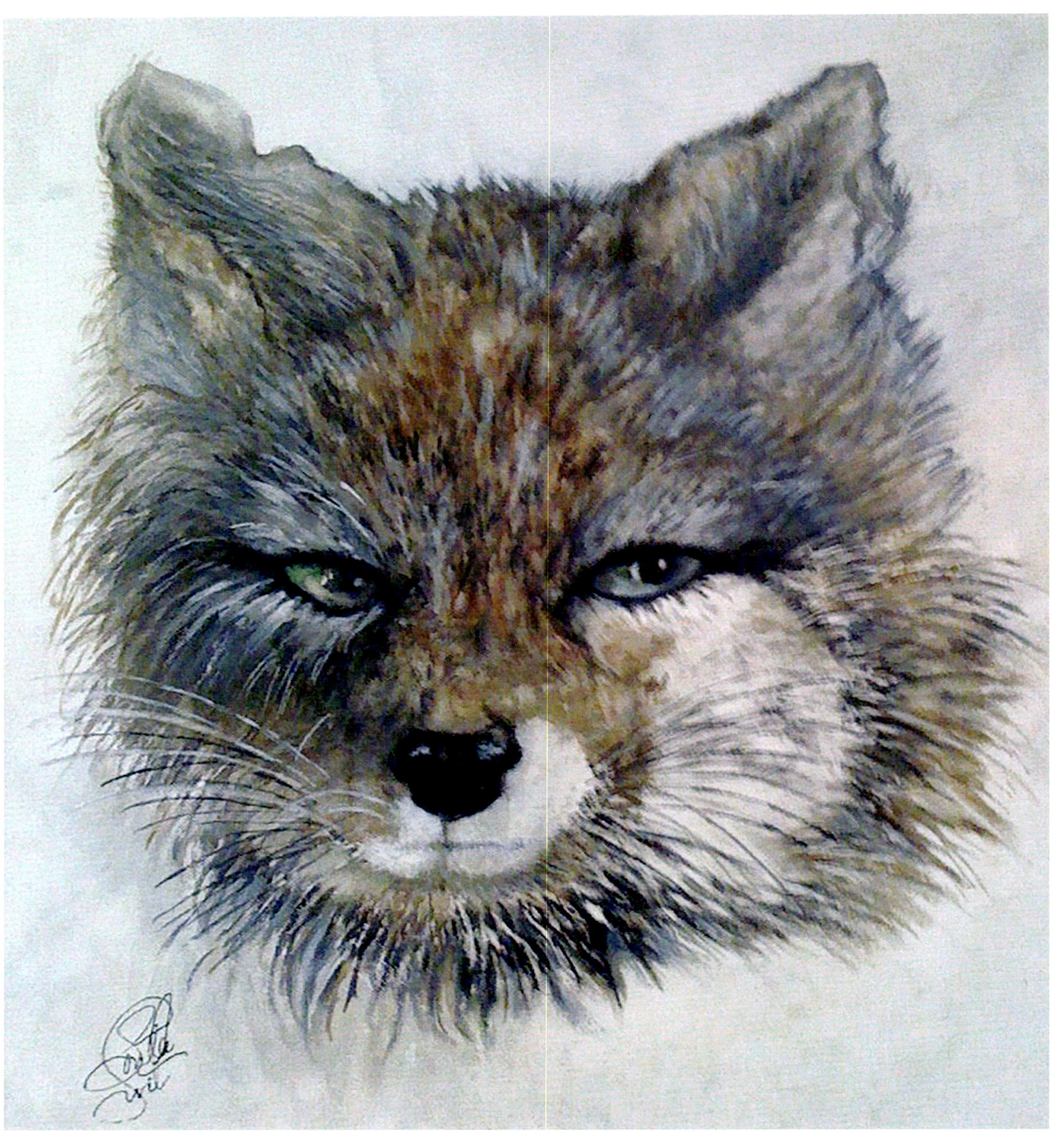

WOLF

My dear friend, John, was an incredible artist and did much to encourage my painting. 'Wolf' is the work I am most proud of. I love those eyes and that snowy chin. John made me aware of seeing all things in shapes. He suggested that I sketch "Piaf," my little Pekingese puppy. I thought it too difficult and way beyond something I could attempt. He asked me what shape I saw when I looked at her. 'Square,' I said, and those few words from John pushed me into a major breakthrough in my artwork. I did a sketch of "Piaf" (right) which John framed immediately.

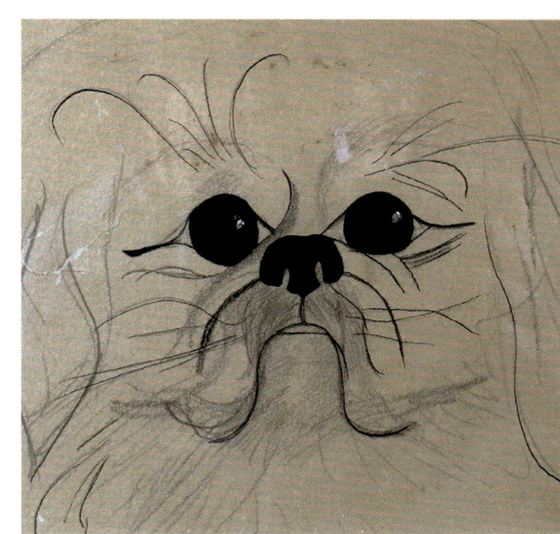

I have it still and I cherish the memory of my dear, talented friend.

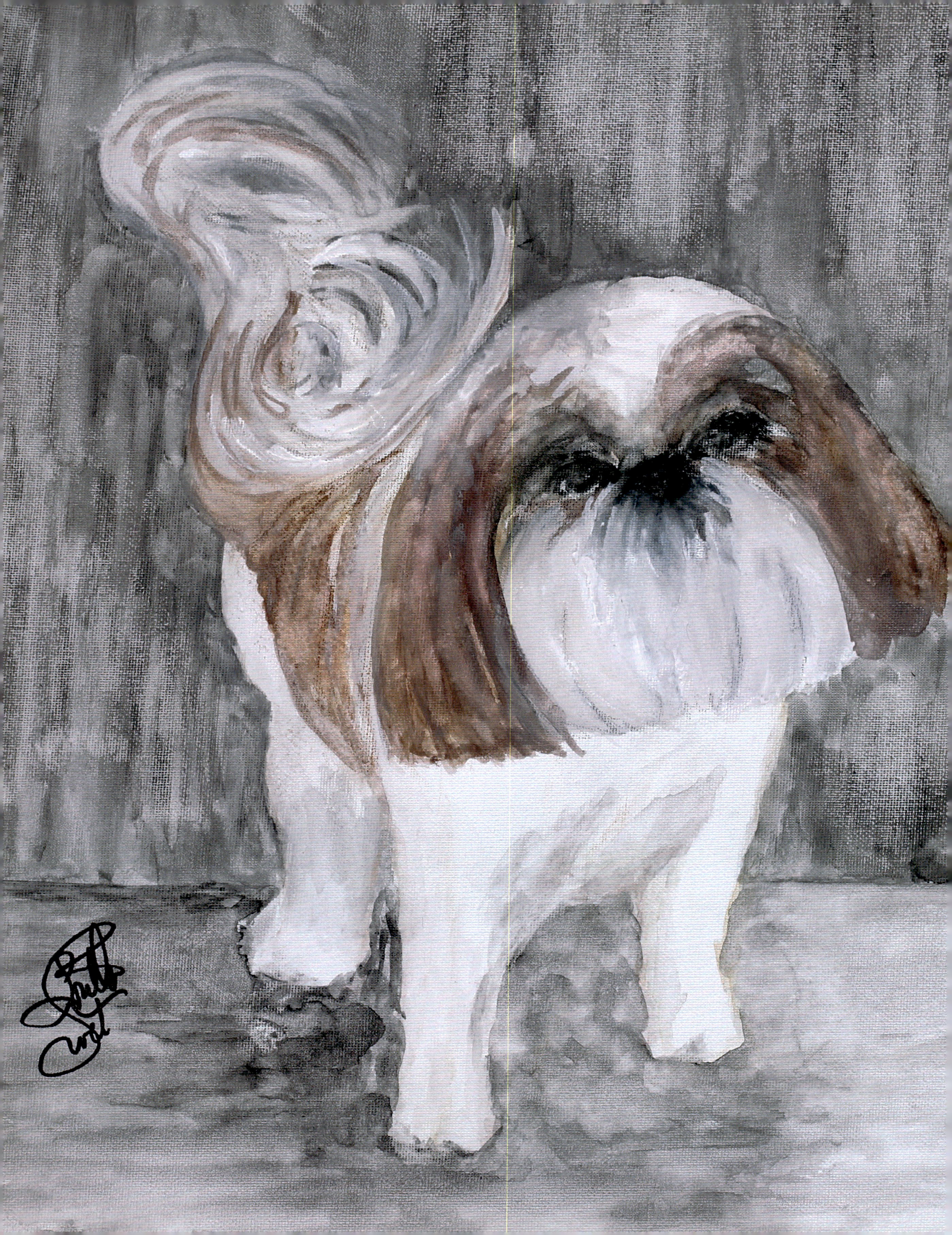

SOPHIE

Sophie, Sophie, Sophie. Straight from a fluffing at the beauty salon and ready for her 'photo-op.' This little darling was not at all spoiled. She just happens to look like a centerfold. We had a great photo session, giving me a lush array of pictures from which to choose for the definitive, quintessential Sophie. I couldn't resist the 'movement' of that fluffy tail. Sophie......... you rock!

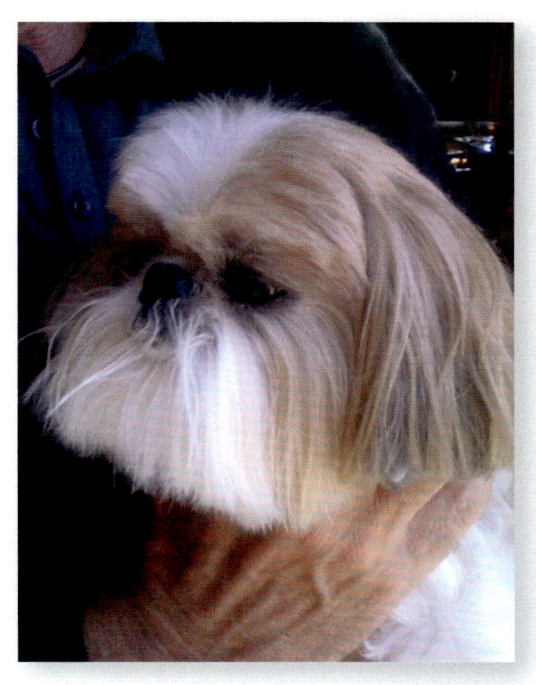

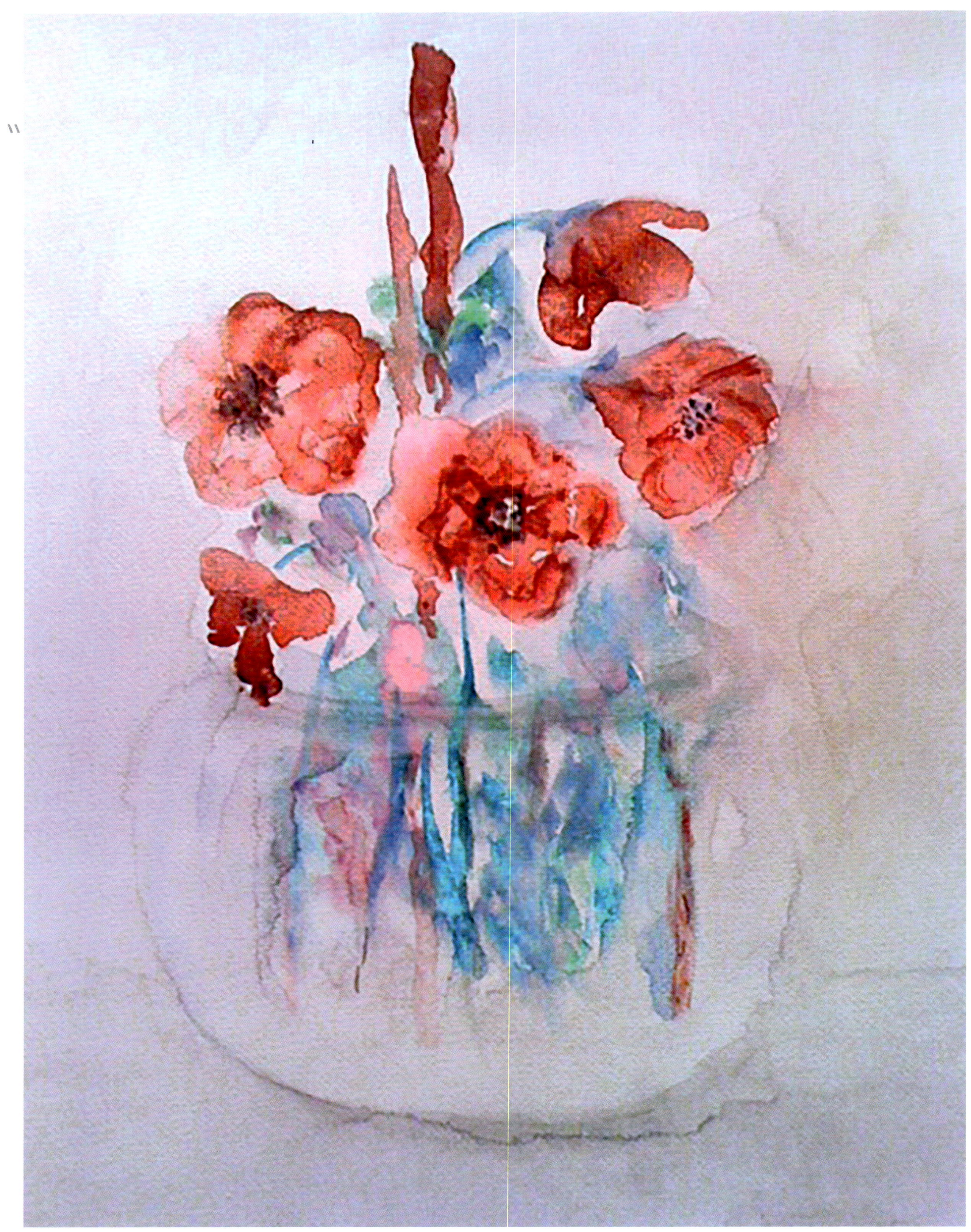

RED POPPIES

Canada is great — I love working there, onstage or in film. The audiences are so appreciative; the people are so friendly. Take, for example, dear Helen and Gene Bidinot.

While I was performing "Shirley Valentine" in Ontario, they included me in all their family gatherings. When I left for New York, they rearranged their schedule so that we could make the trip together.

As it happens, Gene's business is the Bonanza Garden Centre. What could be more natural than to paint a floral for them with gratitude for their kindness.

TEDDY

A lot of pleasure comes from surprising a humane advocate with a painting of their beloved animal companion. Teddy, a surprise for Jim Korinke, was one such highlight for me.

In addition to sharing our passion for animals, I had had the privilege of sharing a stage with him in two exceptional productions at the New Theatre.

Jim is enormously talented with an acting range as wide as the Grand Canyon. Off-stage and in the wings, he's an utter delight, with his second career of rescuing and placing animals in loving, forever homes.

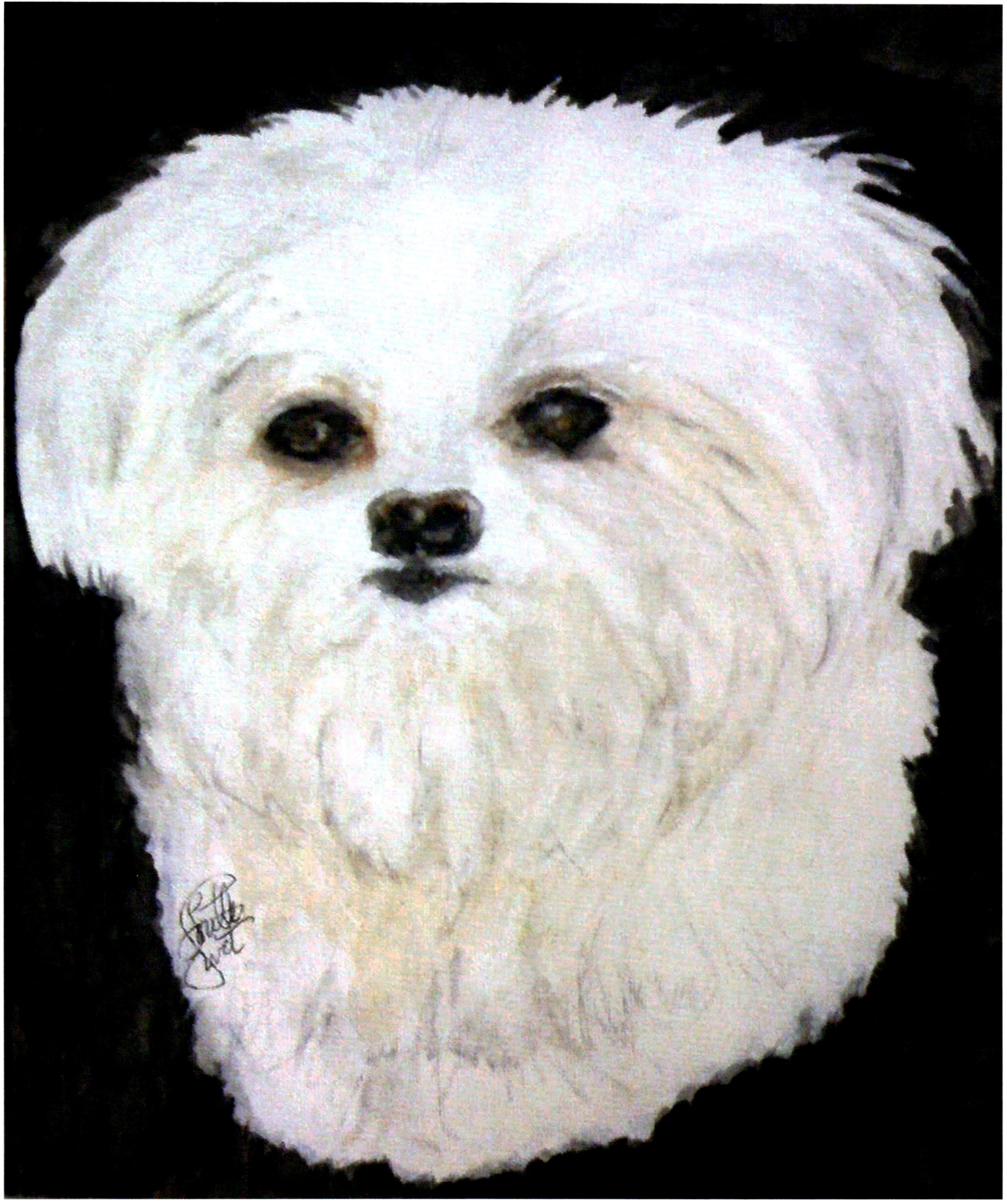

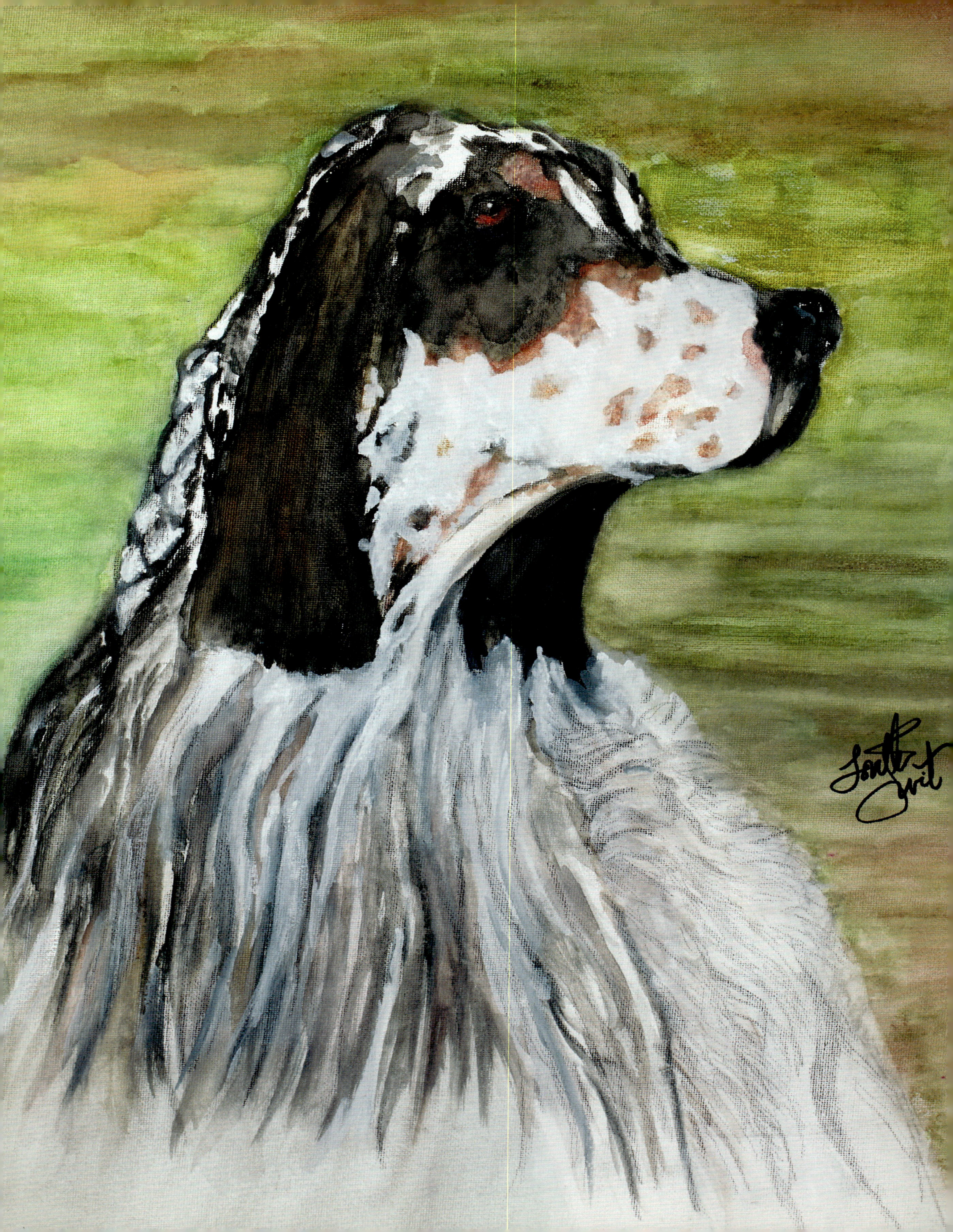

SASHA

Sasha is an English Setter and a beauty. I saw her photo in a calendar and had an immediate 'must-do' reaction. She was the second painting to blossom in that most beautiful setting high above Windsor, Canada, when I was on tour with 'Love/Loss/Wore.'

I'm grateful to the Ephrons for that delightful play, and I'm grateful to my producer, Daryl Roth, not only for her high standards and impeccable taste, but also for the dedication and support she gives to the humane cause.

HIS MAJESTY CHARLES (AND THE PROCESS)

I was on tour, and in Detroit, staying in the perfect setting for some serious artwork. With floor-to-ceiling windows, the light was magnificent. When I'm working onstage at night, I love having the time and freedom to paint all afternoon. I took some photos of "His Majesty" as he developed. That's always so interesting, watching the subject come to life. At this point I began to challenge myself, working with a larger canvas. That hotel suite, overlooking Windsor, provided not only a beautiful view, but also wonderful light and inspiration.

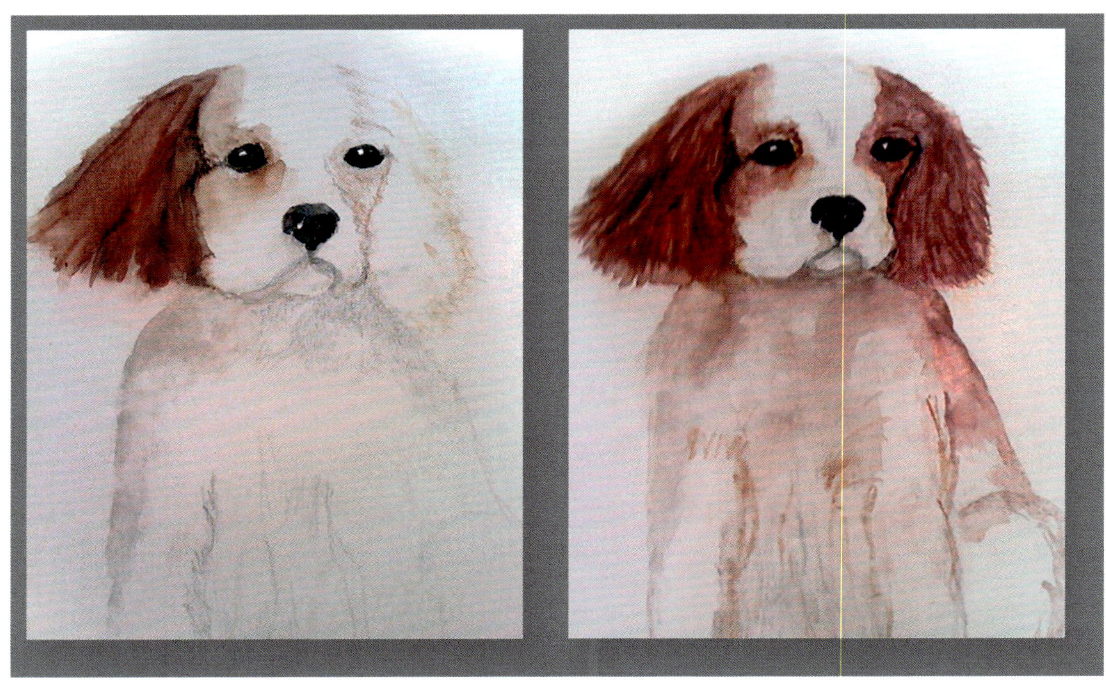

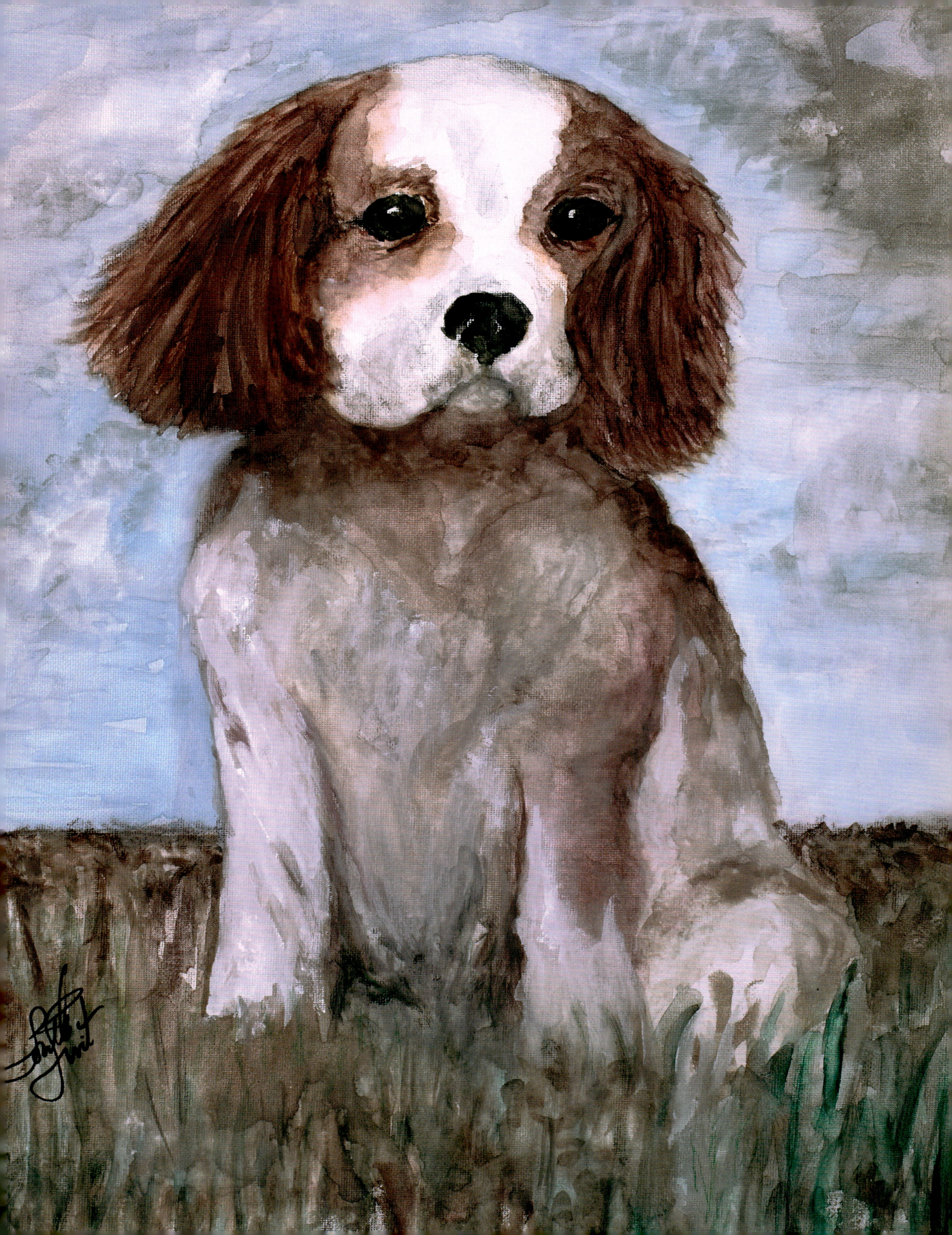

HEAVENLY RABBITS

I was approached to do this painting as a gift for a retiring Board member of a humane organization. Her beloved rabbit, now deceased, had been a great love in her life. She wept openly when the framed painting was presented to her at the event of her retirement. She saw what I saw. Her beloved pet rabbit in heavenly clouds with shadows of other angelic rabbits......... comforting.

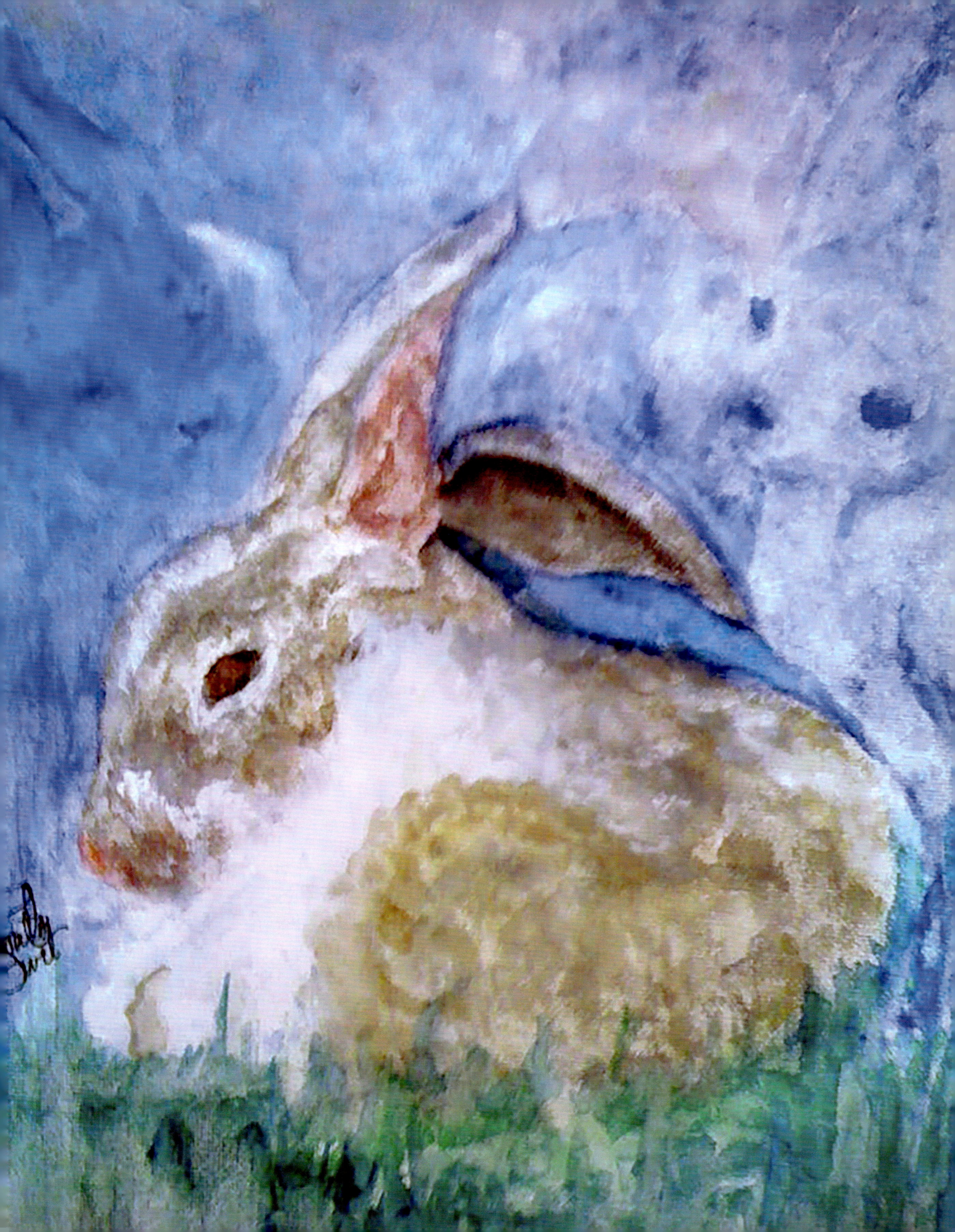

BABY NEW YORKIE®

I'm prejudiced, okay? What can I say? Alright, I'm biased. This is my beloved little "Munchkin" – known to my bilingual friends as "Charamusca." Don't ask......... The name has no real meaning. It's a Spanish dessert, I'm told, like our saying a fudge sundae as it were or an eclair.

It is what it is. It's a "Charamusca." Irresistible. Adorable. Delicious. She's a New York-ie®. Loves The Big Apple.

Her best friend is Schmitty, the Weather Dog......... Don't ask.........

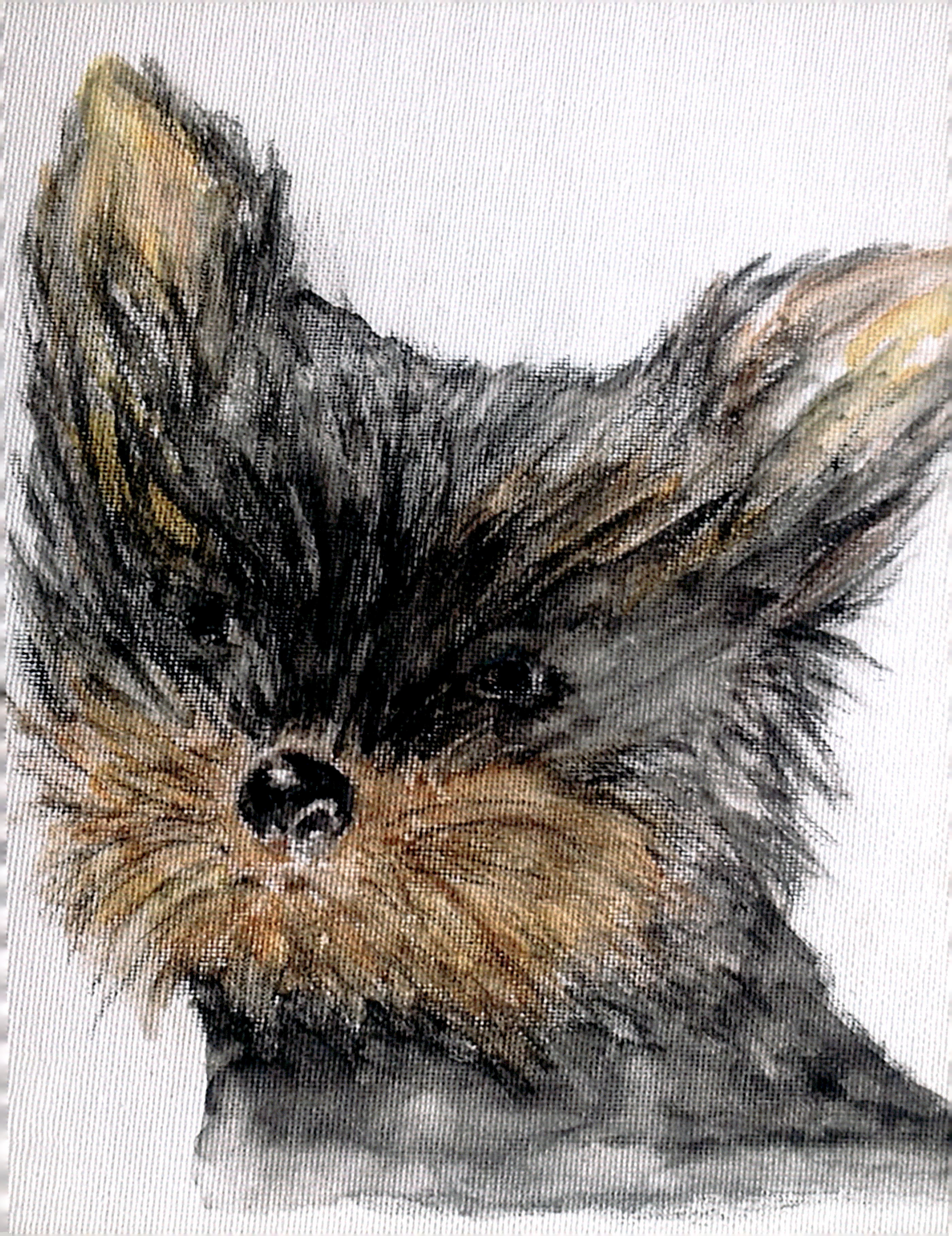

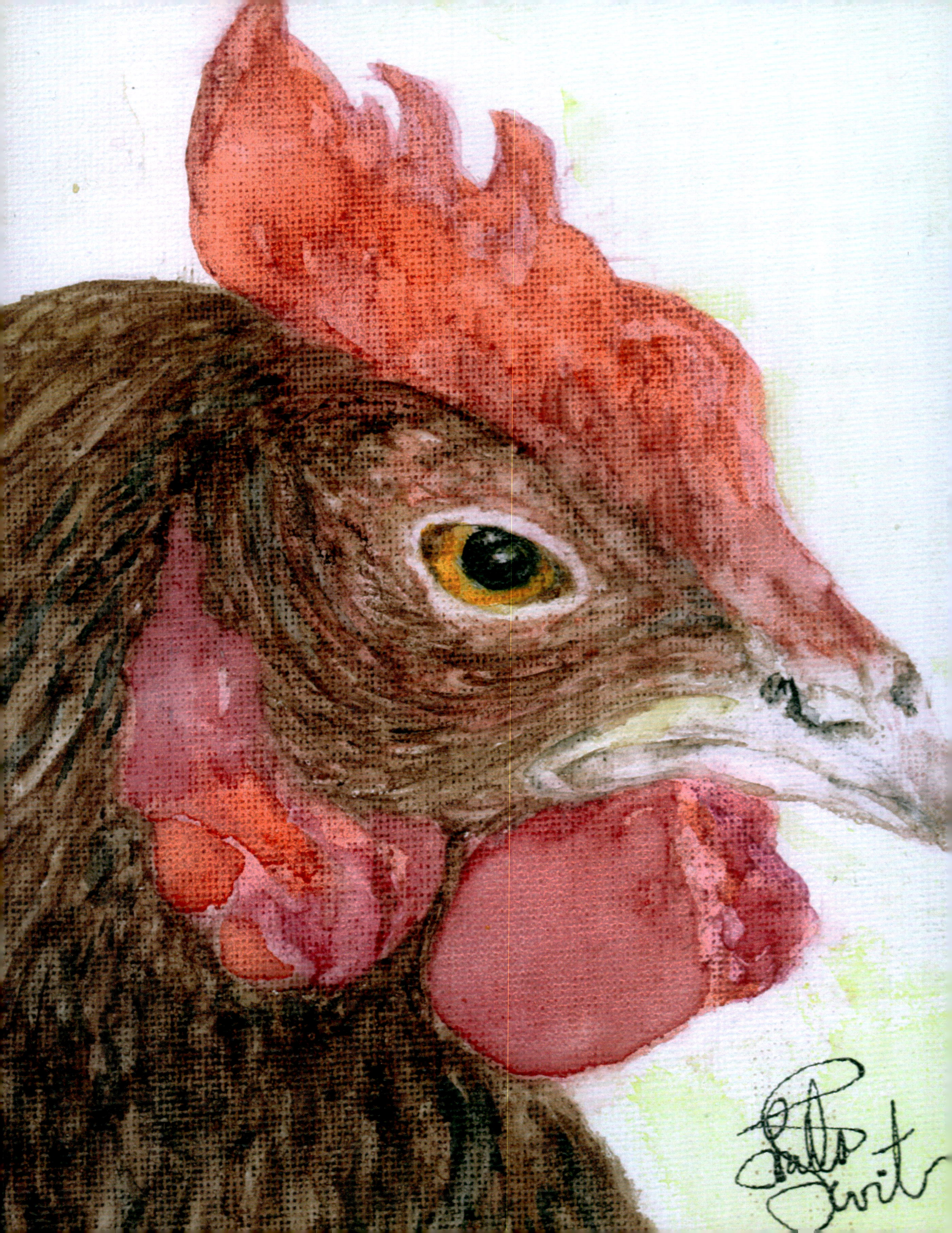

MAESTRO

Ooooooooo, "chicken skin." Remember saying that when you were a child? Sometimes you'd feel like that, watching a wonderful old black and white Frankenstein movie. Your skin would prune and pickle.

What I most love about Maestro is his raspy, bumpy skin. Probably a point of pride for a rooster......... who knows. I am just so delighted with the way he turned out.

Ooooooooo! It gives me "chicken skin."

SUMATRA

Slender, slinky, sensual......... there is nothing quite so sensational as the exotic beauty of the Big Cats. Their grace, their muscular frame, their balletic coordination......... they are one of nature's expressions of perfection.

Sumatra lived out her life at the wonderful WILDLIFE WAYSTATION, surrounded by friends who respected and cared for her lovingly.

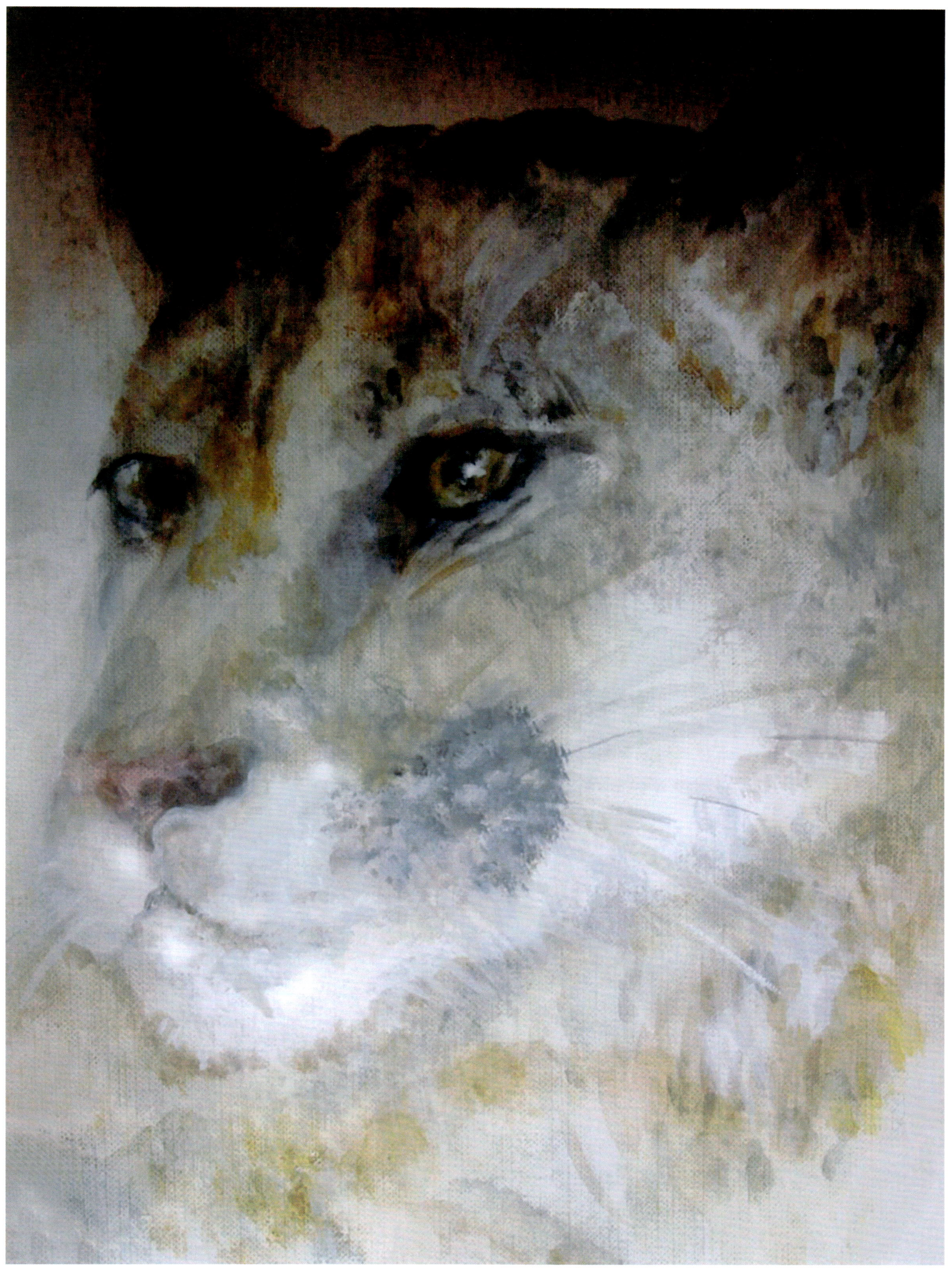

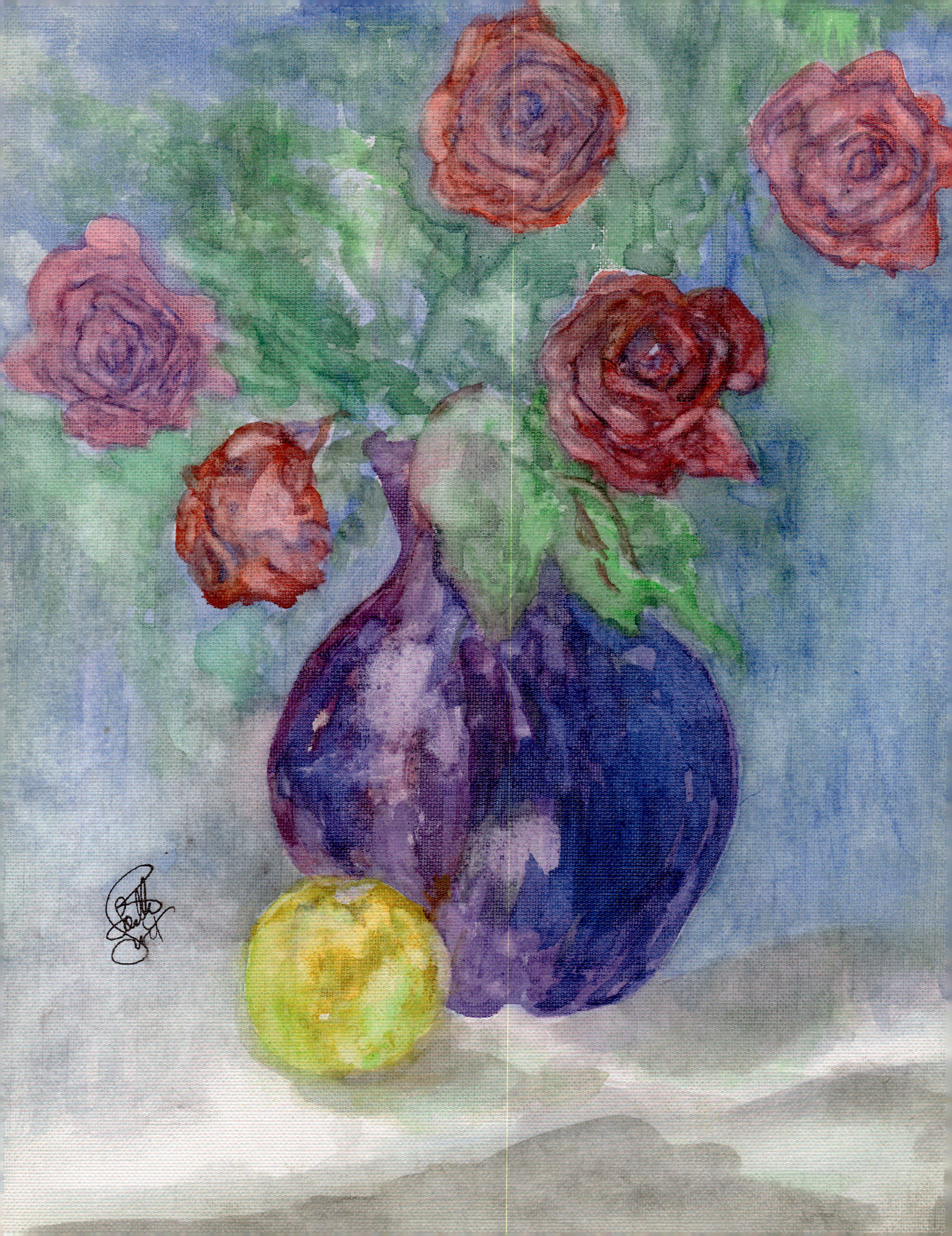

ROSES ARE RED

My head was leaning way back in the dentist chair. It was nothing painful, a systematic, often boring, cleaning session with the hygienist. My eyes, scanning the room, fell on a colorful, very pretty floral print, hanging on the wall, blooming with three favorite colors: red, red, and red.

I tried to keep it in view while keeping my face at the angle set by the hygienist. We both did our best. My guess is that my effort does not remotely resemble that lovely print in the office; I love the red, the leaves, the red, the fruit and the red!!"

FIONA

Fiona was a commission from Margaret Fishback and what a delight! I never had the pleasure and fun to meet the genuine article, but truth be known, the painting is of Fiona as a puppy. It was that sweet baby pup they wanted to preserve in watercolor.

I fell totally in love, and the challenges seemed to dissipate as she unfolded on the canvas. Painting her 'baby' portrait was one of the best times I've ever had.

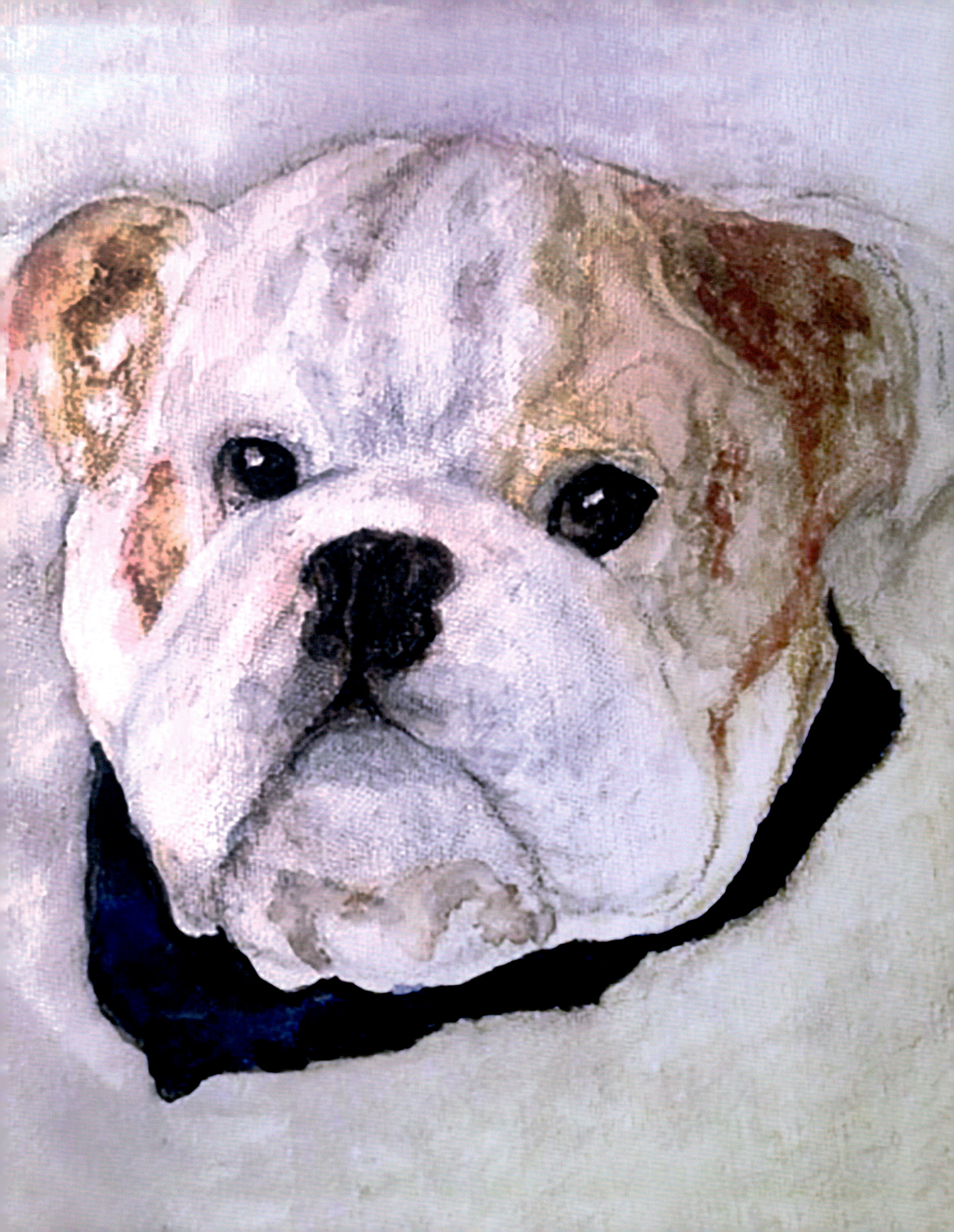

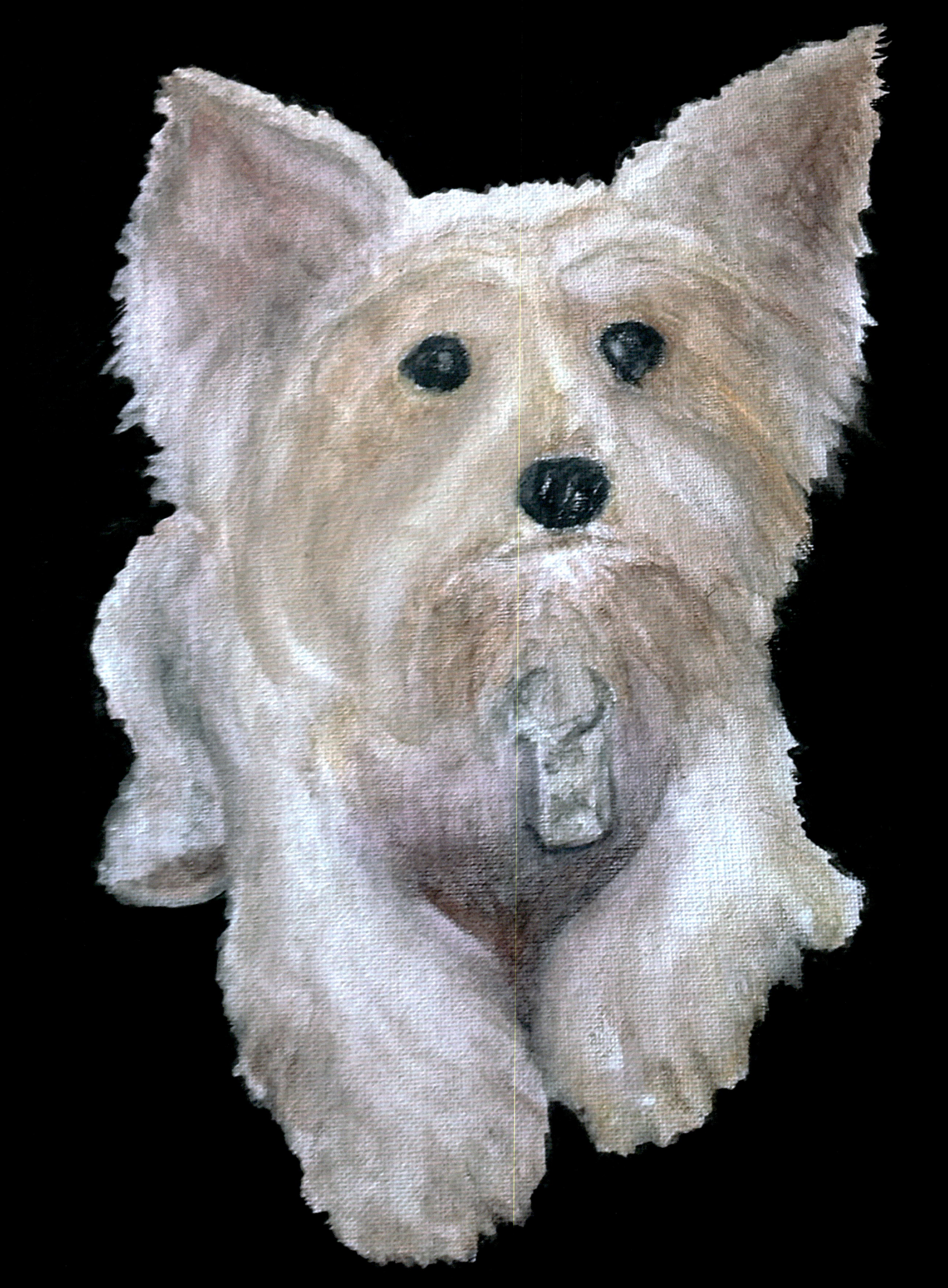

JOE

"Max" was re-christened "Joe" because the resemblance was too startling to do otherwise. Joe he is, undeniably, and his human companion 'parents' bought a Gicle print immediately, the funds from same going to AYLA'S ACRES where I retain an Honorable Board membership.

We were eventing a fundraiser at Ayla's Thrift Shop when we discovered the remarkable similarity between "Joe" and "Max." The funds, by any other name, still goes towards supporting Ayla's. Perhaps I should paint another pose of Max though.

Don't want to step on any paws..........

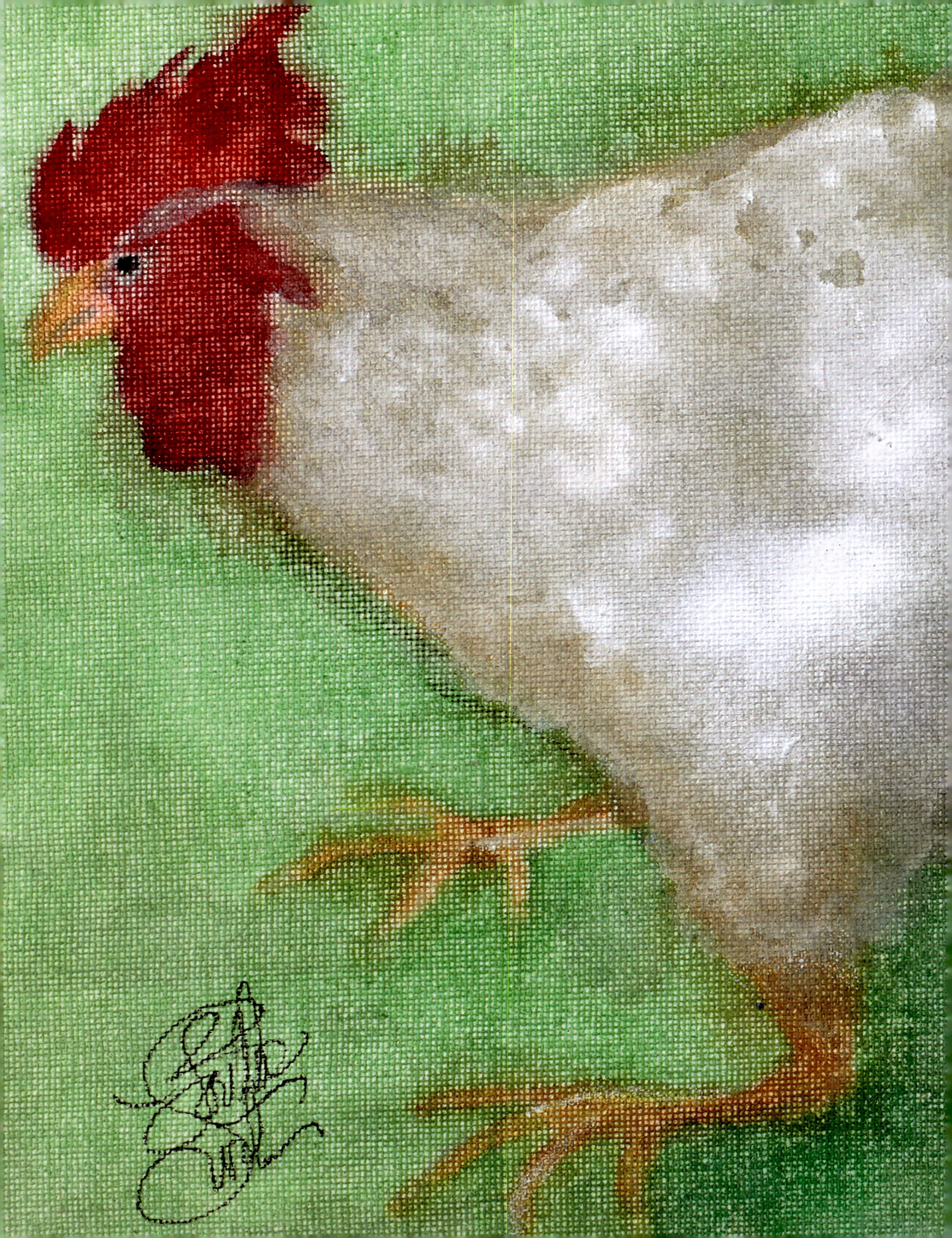

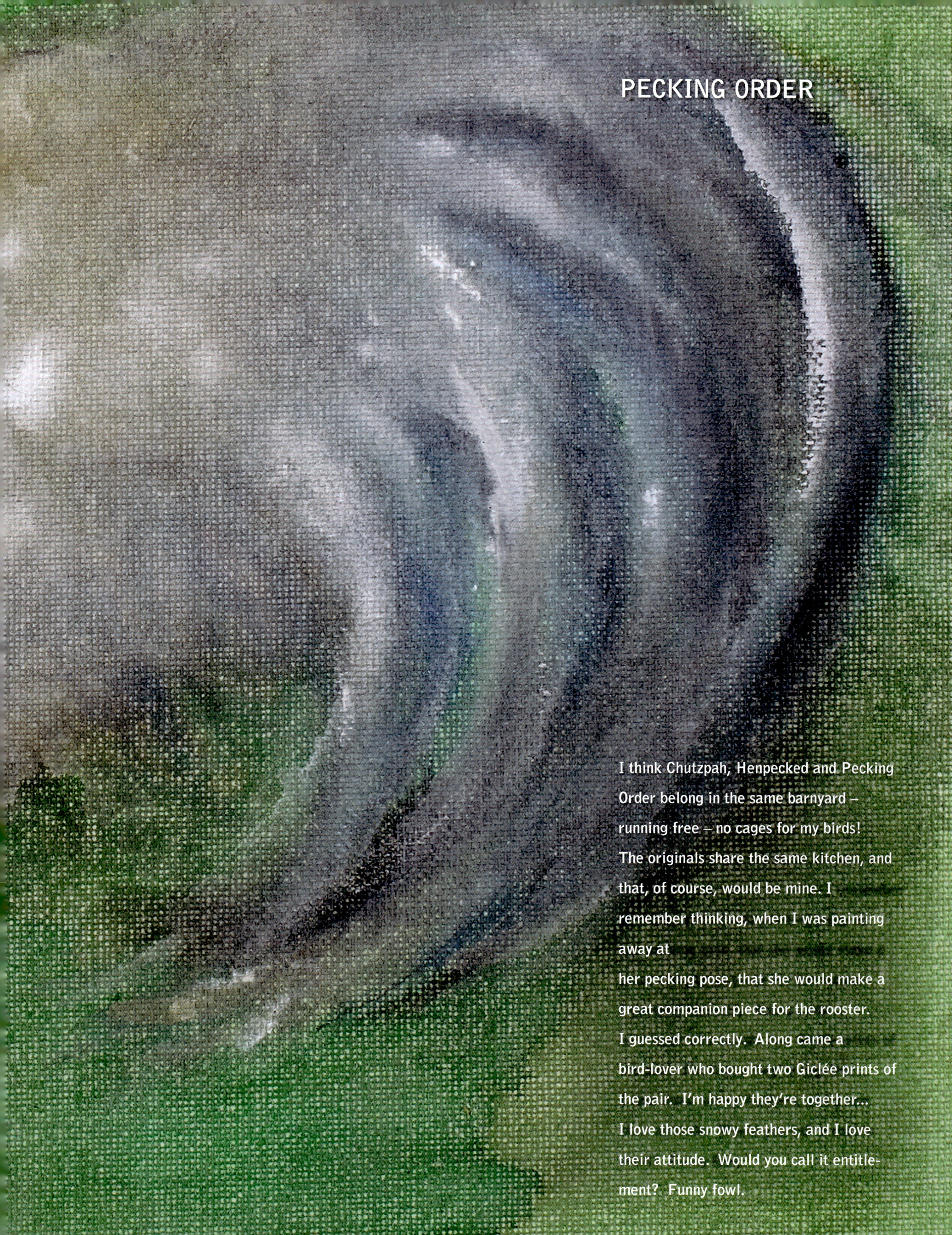

PECKING ORDER

I think Chutzpah, Henpecked and Pecking Order belong in the same barnyard – running free – no cages for my birds! The originals share the same kitchen, and that, of course, would be mine. I remember thinking, when I was painting away at

her pecking pose, that she would make a great companion piece for the rooster. I guessed correctly. Along came a bird-lover who bought two Giclée prints of the pair. I'm happy they're together... I love those snowy feathers, and I love their attitude. Would you call it entitlement? Funny fowl.

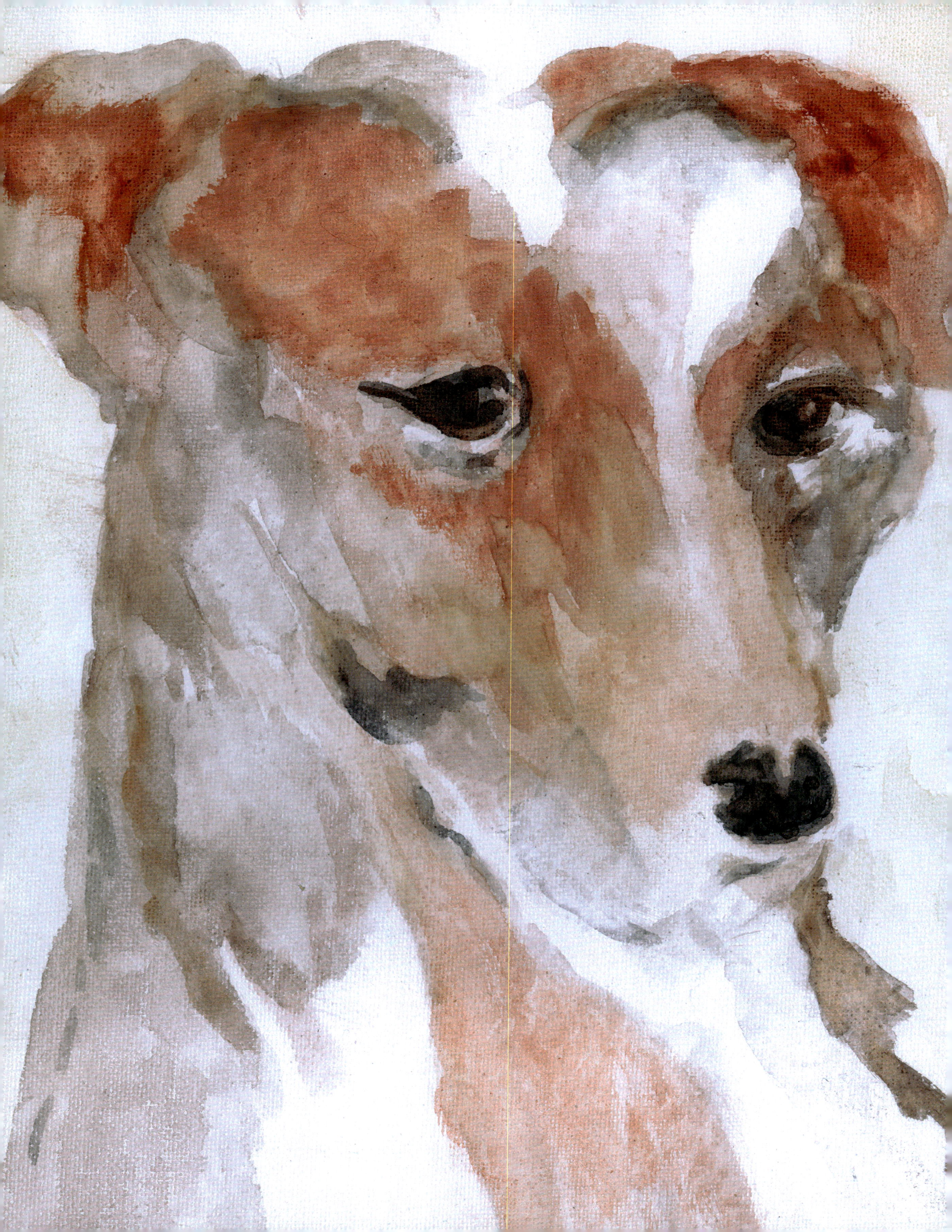

STYLIZED JACK RUSSELL

I've painted portraits of quite a few Jack Russells, for starters, the book's cover, that sweet BIDE-A-WEE rescue. Here is a somewhat 'stylized' Jack Russell painting I wanted to include. It was the favorite of my wonderful friend and colleague, Wayne Rogers. I was complimented always by his flattering, positive critique of my artwork.

Wayne was known for his impeccable taste, and as most people know, he was something of a Mensa in the financial world, doling out investment opinions on weekly broadcasts.

Losing such a dear friend was painful.

I'll miss him always.

GOLIATH

A sweet, gentle giant. Years ago Golilath was at AYLA'S ACRES, just "hangin' out." There's such an air of protection this breed seems to telegraph. Those big brown eyes hold such a promise of safety. I love the casual air he has of just checking it all out......... making certain all is well.

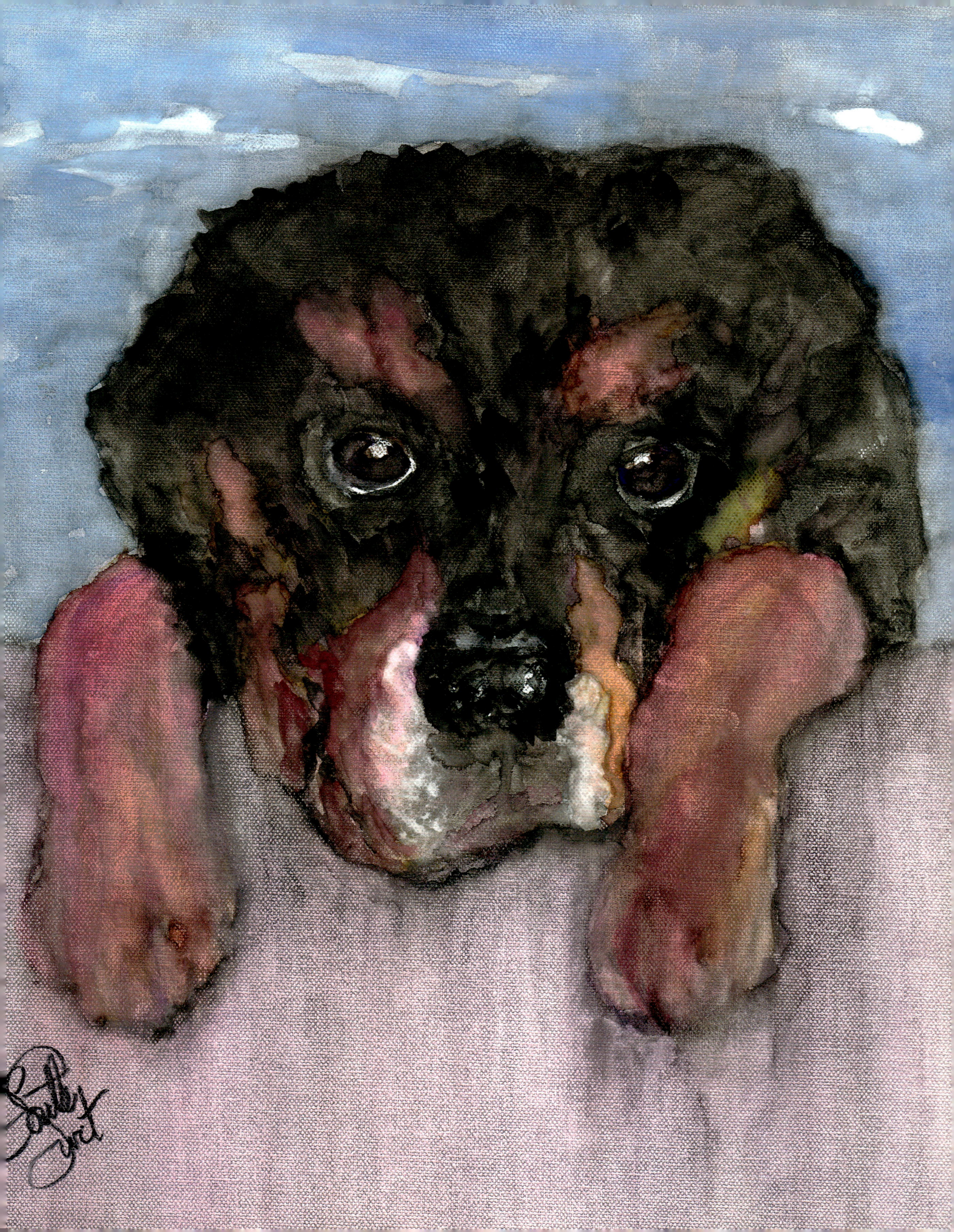

CONAN

Conan started out as a doodle on a telephone message pad and matured into a very wonderful painting.

There is a dignity and gentleness about him. He lived at the WILDLIFE WAYSTATION. One day during a Waystation tour, some youngsters asked if Conan belonged to Arnold Schwarzenegger. When they were told not, they suggested we make certain that Arnold be told that Conan lived there. So Martine Collette, founder, did just that. In response, Arnold sent a donation to cover Conan's expenses for a year.

How nice......... thanks, Arnold.

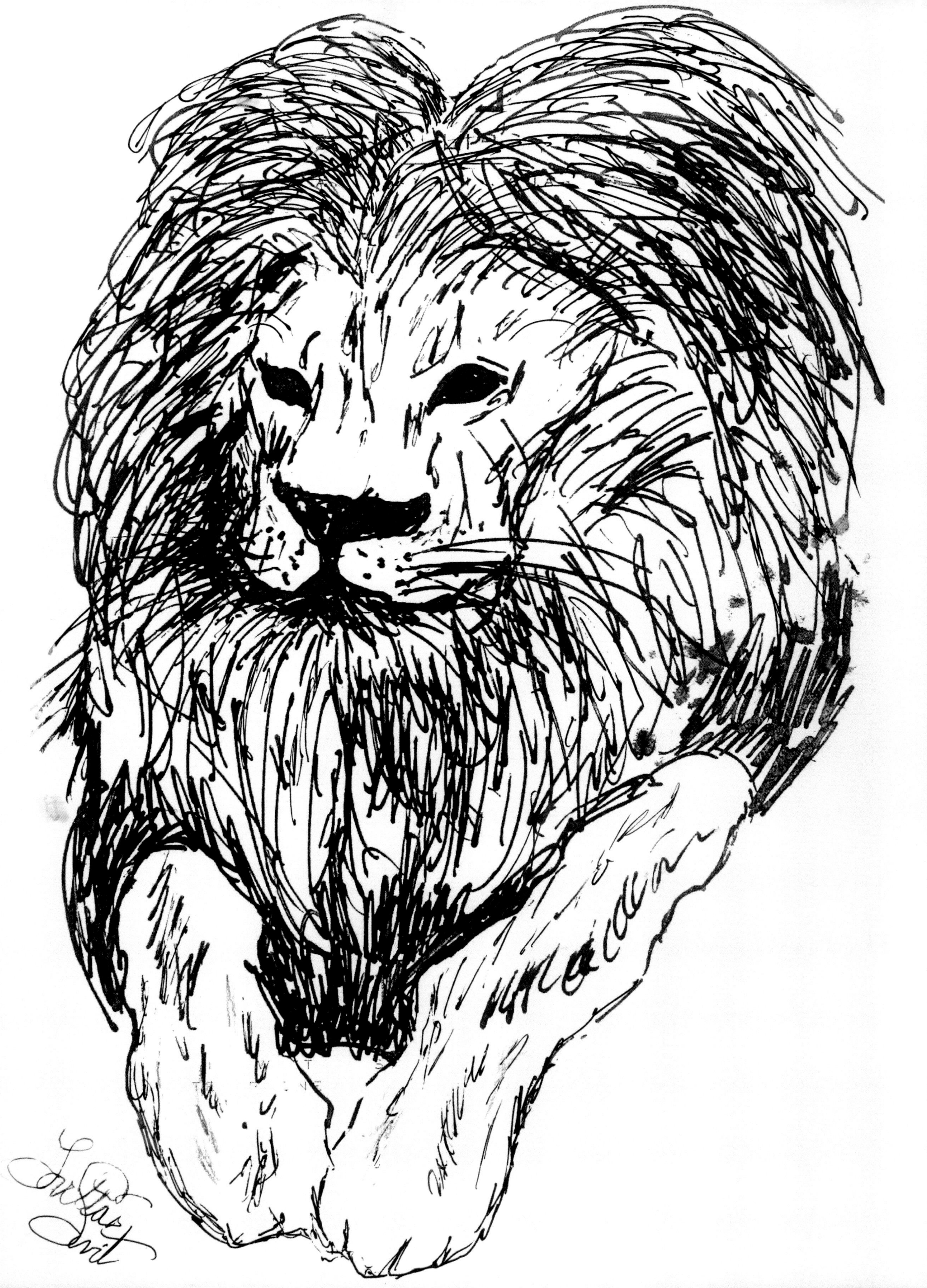

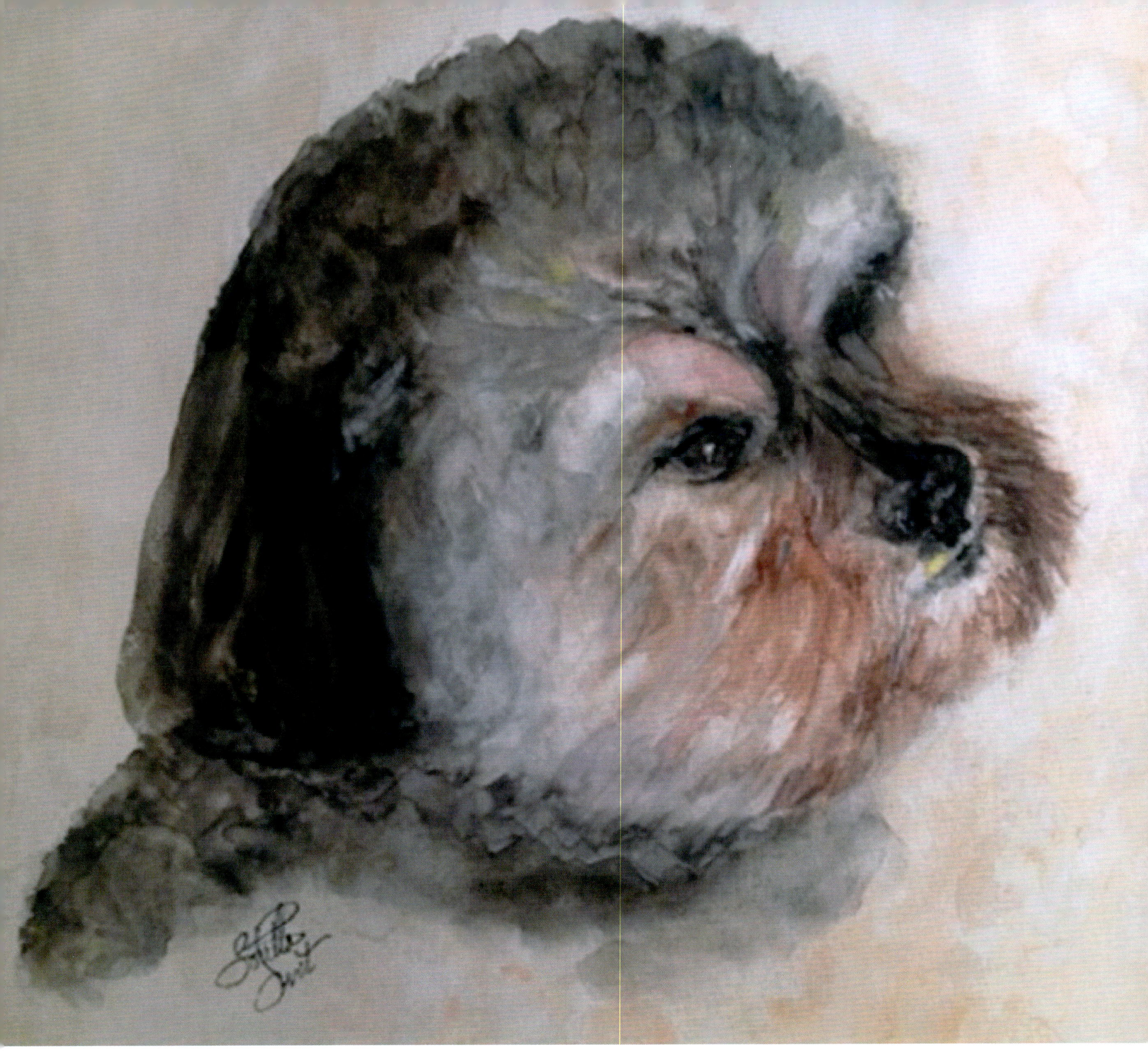

PEPPER

No other name could have been more appropriate for this cute little rescue. He looked like he'd been sprinkled with coarse-ground black and white pepper. We were having a fund-raising event at the AYLA'S ACRES THRIFT STORE in St. Augustine, Florida, when Jimmy, the young man who adopted Pepper, approached me to commission a painting.

He and his mother were frequent shoppers at the Shop. This time he came with a variety of photos of Pepper. Painting Pepper was great fun. Jimmy loved the result.

Spicy!

ORGANIZATIONS WORKING TIRELESSLY AND RELENTLESSLY WITH MS. SWIT TO END ANIMAL SUFFERING AND CRUELTY.

Actors and Others for Animals
1523 Burbank Boulevard
North Hollywood, CA 91601
www.actorsandothers.com

Ayla's Acres No-Kill Animal Rescue & Thriftique
413 Anastasia Blvd.
St. Augustine, FL 32080
www.aylasacres.org

Bide-a-Wee
152 West 24th Street
New York, NY 10011
www.bidawee.org
donate@bideawee.org

Farm Sanctuary
IN CALIFORNIA
5200 Escondido Canyon Road
Acton, CA 93510
IN NEW YORK:
3100 Aikens Road
Watkins Glen, NY 14891
www.farmsanctuary.org
info@farmsanctuary.org

The Fur-Bearers
(Association for the Protection of Fur-Bearing Animals)
Vancouver, Canada
www.thefurbearers.com
info@thefurbearers.com

Hooved Animal Rescue and Protection (HARPS)
P.O. Box 94
Barrington, IL 60011-0094
info@harpsonline.org

The Humane League
1601 Walnut Street,
Suite 502
Philadelphia, PA 19102
info@thehumaneleague.com

The Humane Society of the United States
1255 23rd Street NW,
Suite 450 Washington,
DC 20037
donorcare@humanesociety.org

International Fund for Animal Welfare (IFAW)
290 Summer Street
Yarmouth Port, MA 02675
www.ifaw.org
info@ifaw.org

Israel Guide Dog Center
IN PENNSYLVANIA
968 Easton Rd – Suite H
Warrington, PA 18976
info@israelguidedog.org
www.israelguidedog.org
IN ISRAEL
Ha'Sadot 6
Beit Oved 7680000, ISRAEL
info@igdcb.org
www.he.israelguidedog.org

The Kaua'i Humane Society
3-825 Kaumualii Hwy
PO Box 3330 (mailing)
Lihue, HI 96766
support@kauaihumane.org
www.kauaihumane.org

Mission K9 Rescue
Serving Working Dogs Around The World
PO Box 395
Needville, TX 77461-0395
www.MissionK9Rescue.org
MissionK9Rescue@gmail.com

MSPCA
350 South Huntington Avenue
Boston, MA 02130
webeditor@mspca.org
angell.org | mspca.org

Pets for Vets
P. O. 10860
Wilmington, NC 28404
www.petsforvets.com
info@petsforvets.com

Search Dog Foundation (SDF)
6800 Wheeler Canyon Road
Santa Paula, CA 93060
www.searchdogfoundation.org

Tabby Town Cat Adoption
Center McKinley Mall
3701 McKinley Parkway
Blasdell, NY 14219
info@tabbytown.org

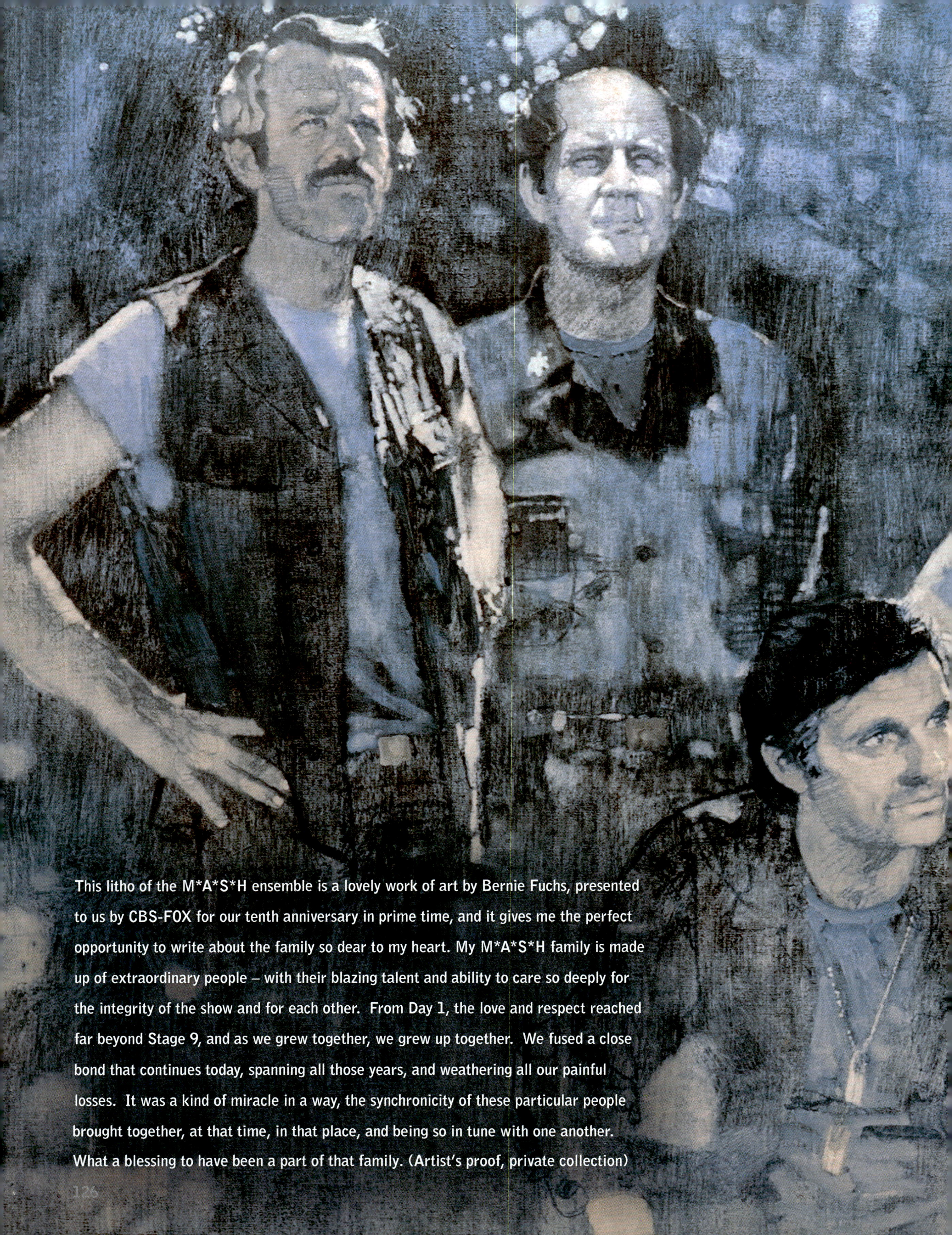

This litho of the M*A*S*H ensemble is a lovely work of art by Bernie Fuchs, presented to us by CBS-FOX for our tenth anniversary in prime time, and it gives me the perfect opportunity to write about the family so dear to my heart. My M*A*S*H family is made up of extraordinary people – with their blazing talent and ability to care so deeply for the integrity of the show and for each other. From Day 1, the love and respect reached far beyond Stage 9, and as we grew together, we grew up together. We fused a close bond that continues today, spanning all those years, and weathering all our painful losses. It was a kind of miracle in a way, the synchronicity of these particular people brought together, at that time, in that place, and being so in tune with one another. What a blessing to have been a part of that family. (Artist's proof, private collection)

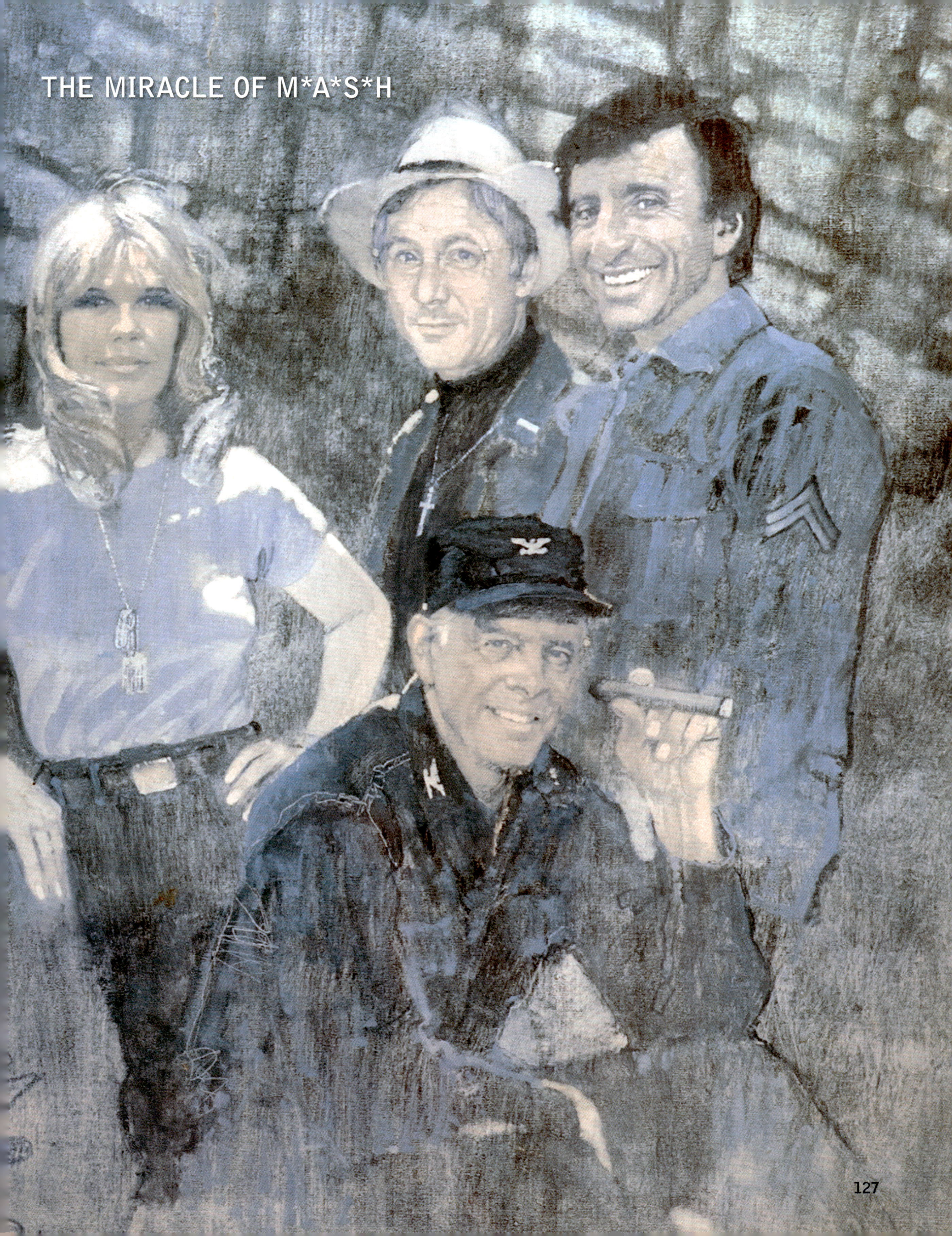

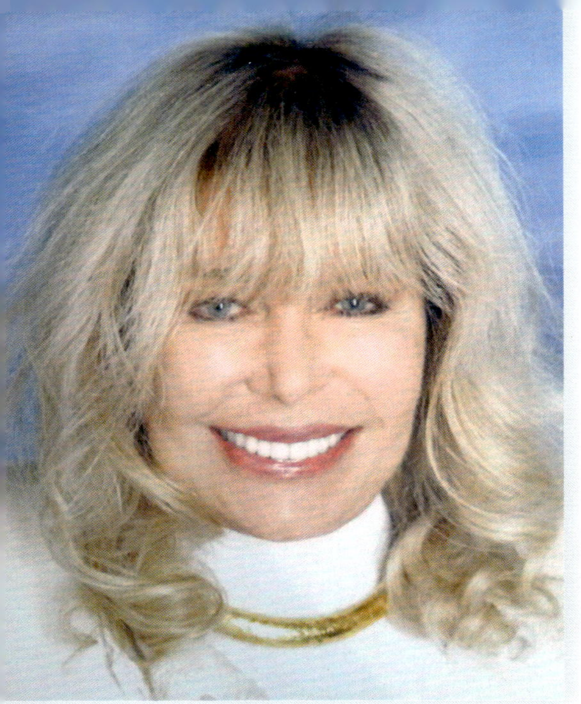

A CAREER OF HIGHLIGHTS

Loretta Swit has devoted much of her time to animal-related causes and is a strong advocate for animals and animal rights. Following are some highlights from her career as a beloved and consummate performer.

1965–1967 Toured with the national company of 'Any Wednesday', then appeared in the 'Odd Couple' opposite Don Rickles and Ernest Borgnine in California, and in Florida opposite E.G. Marshall and Shelly Berman.

1968–1969 Played 'Agnes Gooch' opposite two Oscar-winning 'Mames': Celeste Holm on the tour, and Susan Hayward in Caesars Palace, Las Vegas.

1969–1971 Segued from Nevada to Los Angeles where she starred in guest roles for such prime-time series as: Gunsmoke, Hawaii Five-0, Mission Impossible, and Mannix.

1971–1983 Won the role of Maj. Margaret 'Hot Lips' Houlihan in television's most honored series, M*A*S*H, which elevated her and her co-stars to iconic status. Only she and Alan Alda remained for the entire eleven seasons of the run.

1972–1990 M*A*S*H filmed more than 250 episodes during its eleven seasons. During breaks from filming, Ms. Swit starred in some 25 television movies and 8 feature films. She received 10 Emmy Award nominations and 4 for the Golden Globe Award.

1976–1977 Starred on Broadway in 'Same Time, Next Year' opposite Ted Bessell, and again with Don Murray, repeating the role opposite John O'Hurley in Canada.

1981 Created the role of 'Christine Cagney' in the television movie of Cagney & Lacey, with contractual obligations to M*A*S*H precluding her continuing the role in the tv series.

Specials Guested on the Muppet Show; the Bob Hope Christmas Show; Perry Como's Special in the Bahamas; the Donny and Marie Osmond Special; Bob Hope's Pre-Olympic Special in Korea; the PBS Special: A Christmas Calendar; Saving the Wildlife; The Mae West Story; and Korea The Forgotten War.

1989 Received a star on the Hollywood Boulevard Walk of Fame.

1991 Was given the Sarah Siddons Award, Chicago's most prestigious honor, for her performance in 'Shirley Valentine', a play she toured across the U.S. and in Canada, giving more than 1,500 performances.

1992 Hosted the Discovery Channel 26-part series Those Incredible Animals.

1993–Present
Appeared in 'The Vagina Monologues' Off-Broadway, New York, and in the West End in London. With Anthony Franciosa, toured in 'Love Letters'. Appeared in 'Love, Loss and What I Wore' Off-Broadway and in Chicago. Narrated the film: 'Never The Same: the POW experience in WWII'.

Ms. Swit is performing in regional theaters or on tour in plays including 'Eleanor–Her Secret Journey', 'Me and Jezebel', and 'Six Dance Lessons in Six Weeks'.

Loretta Swit continues to captivate audiences, all the while pursuing her passion for the arts, her unending philanthropic work, and her relentless campaign against cruelty.

AWARDS

4 Golden Globe Nominations: 1974, 1980, 1982, 1983
10 EMMY Award Nominations EMMY Awards: 1980, 1982
Genie Award, American Women in Radio and Television (AWRT) Silver Satellite Award (AWRT-Canada) The Peoples Choice Award, 1983 Star on Hollywood Walk of Fame, 1989 The Sarah Siddons Award, 1991 (Chicago Theatre highest honor) The Jean Golden Halo Award
The Pioneer Broadcasters Award
Woman of the Year Award (International Fund for Animal Welfare, IFAW)
Woman of the Year Award, API
The Advocate for Farm Animals Award, 2007 (The Farm Sanctuary)
TV Land Impact Award, 2009
Compassion in Action Award (Ayla's Acres)
Career Achievement Award (Film Festival Ft. Lauderdale)
Westminster Animal Welfare & Leadership Award
Red Cross Humanitarian Award, 2016
Global Wildlife Conservation Champion Award, 2016 (GES Africa Conservation Fund)
Polish Artist Achievement Award, 2016
The Betty White Award, 2016 (Actors and Others for Animals)